MW01099031

Addition & Subtraction Facts to 20

Over 80 Puzzles and Games

Written by Joellyn Cicciarelli and Sue Lewis

Editor: Christine Hood

Illustrator: Patty Briles

Cover Designer: Barbara Peterson

Designer: Pam Thomson

Project Director: Carolea Williams

Table of Contents

Introduction

Addition & Subtraction Facts to 20 includes over 80 skill-packed puzzles and games that will engage and challenge children at school or at home. Each activity targets and reinforces specific addition and subtraction facts while challenging young minds to think logically and solve problems.

About the Book

The activities in this book provide children with hours of fun and stimulating math fact reinforcement. Each puzzle and game includes:

- easy-to-follow directions
- targeted skills and facts
- a logic or problem-solving component
- exciting challenges
- delightful illustrations

The book is organized as follows:

Addition and Subtraction Activities

Each section of activities, numbered from 5 to 20, can be used to reinforce addition and subtraction facts based on the numbers covered in your current math unit. Or, you can use them to review facts throughout the year. Children can complete the activities independently, in pairs, or in small groups.

Games

Each section also includes a fun and challenging game children can play with a partner. Most materials listed are items readily available in your classroom, such as pennies for place markers, dice, playing cards, or dominoes. Some of the games require minimal preparation, such as creating a set of index cards with addition problems. In these cases, you may also use flash cards.

Quizzes

Four quiz pages are included at the back of the book (pages 89–92), which cover the math facts children have learned. These pages include addition and subtraction facts in increments of 0 to 10 and 11 to 20. Completing these quizzes will help children see their progress and success in learning math facts.

Answer Key

The answer key (pages 93–96) provides an easy teacher reference.

Ideas for Using the Puzzles and Games

Whole Class
- Designate one day each week to be "Math Puzzle Day."
- On this day, duplicate multiple copies of the puzzles or games so everyone can participate in the same activity.
- Copy the puzzle or game onto a transparency and use it with an overhead projector to guide children through the activity.

Small Group
- Use puzzles and games with small groups who need extra practice or enrichment.

Individual
- Invite children to use the activities to fill free time when they have finished other class work.
- Make puzzles and games available as "sponge activities"—they can be done during attendance, before recess, or right before the end of the school day.
- Send activities home with children as homework assignments.

Learning Centers
- Organize puzzles and games by placing photocopies in file folders or large envelopes.
- Keep them in a designated box and area.
- Create a sign or bulletin board to designate the "math fact" learning center.

Name _____ Date _____

Flower Power

Add. Match the two flower parts with the same sums. Use crayons to color each match a different color. You will make six matches and need six colors.

Name _____ Date _____

In the Jungle

Add. Then color the sums using the color key. Use any color for spaces without numbers.

5 = green   **4** = brown   **3** = blue   **2** = red   **1** = yellow   **0** = orange

Addition & Subtraction Facts to 20 ©2002 Creative Teaching Press

Name _____ Date _____

Fly a Kite

See who is holding each kite by tracing the string with crayon. Write the answer to the problem in each kite on the line by the child or dog holding it.

Name _____ Date _____

Dominoes Game

Materials
set of dominoes
pencils

How to Play

1. Remove all dominoes from the set with six dots on one half. (A blank domino = 0.) Place the remaining dominoes facedown on the table and mix them up. Draw three dominoes each.

2. **Player A:** Lay down any domino, faceup.

3. **Player B:** Lay down a domino so one end of yours and one end of your partner's adds up to 5.

4. **Player B:** If you cannot make 5, keep taking dominoes from the pile until you can.

5. Keep taking turns, until someone uses all of his or her dominoes. That person wins. If all the dominoes are chosen, and players still have some left over, add each player's dots. The player with the *lower* total wins.

Example:

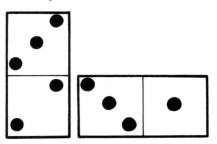

Addition & Subtraction Facts to 20 ©2002 Creative Teaching Press

Name _____ Date _____

Zigzag Sums

Add. Draw a line from each answer in column A to the matching answer in column B. Then draw a line from each answer in column B to the matching answer in column C.

Column A	**Column B**	**Column C**
2 + 0 = _____ ●	● 3 + 3 = _____ ●	● 0 + 2 = _____
3 + 2 = _____ ●	● 1 + 1 = _____ ●	● 5 + 0 = _____
4 + 2 = _____ ●	● 1 + 4 = _____ ●	● 1 + 5 = _____
3 + 1 = _____ ●	● 3 + 0 = _____ ●	● 1 + 3 = _____
2 + 1 = _____ ●	● 2 + 2 = _____ ●	● 1 + 2 = _____

Name _____ Date _____

Beary Square

Look at the number puzzle and see how the lines are shaped around each number. Then "read" the lines below to fill in and solve each problem.

$$\frac{1 \mid 2}{3 \mid 4}$$

Example:

$$1| \; + \; |2 \; = 3$$

1. ___| + |___ = ____

2. |___ + ___| = ____

3. ___| + ___| = ____

4. |‾‾ + ___| = ____

5. ___‾| + |___ = ____

6. ___| + |‾‾ = ____

7. |___ + |___ = ____

8. ___| + |___ = ____

9. |___ + |‾‾ = ____

10. |‾‾ + ‾‾| = ____

Name _____ Date _____

Leap Frog

Subtract. Then find out where the frog hopped by coloring all the lily pads with a difference of 3 or less.

6 − 1 = _____

1 − 1 = _____

6 − 4 = _____

5 − 0 = _____

6 − 0 = _____

4 − 3 = _____

3 − 3 = _____

6 − 2 = _____

5 − 4 = _____

6 − 6 = _____

5 − 1 = _____

2 − 2 = _____

5 − 2 = _____

4 − 2 = _____

4 − 0 = _____

Name _____ Date _____

Roll the Dice Game

Materials
2 dice
score sheet
pencils
calculator or counting beans

How to Play
1. **Player A:** Roll the dice. Subtract the smaller number from the bigger number. Write your number sentence on the score sheet.
2. **Player B:** Take a turn, rolling the dice and subtracting the numbers.
3. Take eight turns each. Add all your answers to get your score, or use a calculator. The player with the *lower* score wins.

Score Sheet	
Player A _____	**Player B** _____
1. _____ – _____ = _____	1. _____ – _____ = _____
2. _____ – _____ = _____	2. _____ – _____ = _____
3. _____ – _____ = _____	3. _____ – _____ = _____
4. _____ – _____ = _____	4. _____ – _____ = _____
5. _____ – _____ = _____	5. _____ – _____ = _____
6. _____ – _____ = _____	6. _____ – _____ = _____
7. _____ – _____ = _____	7. _____ – _____ = _____
8. _____ – _____ = _____	8. _____ – _____ = _____
Score: _____	Score: _____

Name _____ Date _____

Line It Up

Draw lines connecting three numbers to make addition sentences. Start in the far left column, and use the pictures as clues. Write each addition sentence on the lines.

6 + _____ = _____

2 + _____ = _____

0 + _____ = _____

3 + _____ = _____

1 + _____ = _____

5 + _____ = _____

Name _____   Date _____

Fun on the Farm

Add. Then write the sums in the boxes under the problems. To find the answer to each riddle, write the letters that match the answers on the lines below.

3	4	5	6	7
R	M	E	V	O

Riddle: What did the grumpy cow say to the haystack?

1 +3	3 +4	6 +1

2 +4	3 +2

5 +2	3 +3	4 +1	2 +1

" ___ ___ ___ " - ___ ___ ___ ___ ___

0	1	2	3	4	5	6	7
G	O	E	B	N	R	I	H

Riddle: What did the horse say when he moved into the barn?

4 +3	5 +1

2 +2	1 +1	4 +2	0 +0	3 +4

1 +2	0 +1	0 +5

___ ___ " ___ ___ ___ ___ ___ " - ___ ___ ___

Addition & Subtraction Facts to 20 ©2002 Creative Teaching Press

Name _____ Date _____

Number Scramble 7

Choose two numbers in each group to make subtraction sentences. Cross out the two numbers in each group that you did not use.

Example:

2 ✕ 5 ✕

7 - __2__ = __5__

7 - __5__ = __2__

---

4 8 6 3

7 - _____ = _____

7 - _____ = _____

---

3 5 2 3

6 - _____ = _____

6 - _____ = _____

---

3 1 0 4

5 - _____ = _____

5 - _____ = _____

---

4 1 6 2

6 - _____ = _____

6 - _____ = _____

---

3 0 4 2

4 - _____ = _____

4 - _____ = _____

---

1 2 3 0

4 - _____ = _____

4 - _____ = _____

---

0 1 3 2

1 - _____ = _____

1 - _____ = _____

---

3 2 0 1

5 - _____ = _____

5 - _____ = _____

---

2 0 2 3

3 - _____ = _____

3 - _____ = _____

---

1 3 4 1

2 - _____ = _____

2 - _____ = _____

---

3 6 5 1

7 - _____ = _____

7 - _____ = _____

Name _____ Date _____

Treasure Hunt Game

Materials
game board (page 17)
coin
scrap paper
pencils

How to Play

1. **Player A:** Flip a coin. If you get heads, move one space and solve the problem. If you get tails, move two spaces and solve the problem.

2. **Player B:** Check your partner's answer. If it is correct, your partner stays on that space. If it is not correct, your partner moves back one space. Now it's *your* turn to flip the coin and solve a problem.

3. Take turns until a player reaches the treasure chest. The first person to reach the treasure wins!

Addition & Subtraction Facts to 20 ©2002 Creative Teaching Press

Treasure Hunt Game Board

START

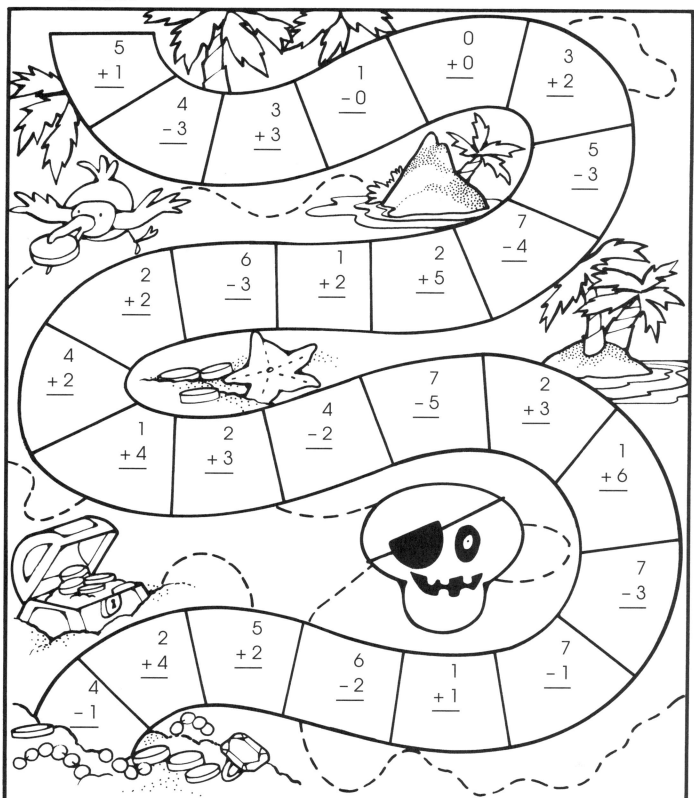

Name _____ Date _____

Funky Four-Square

Look at the number puzzle and see how the lines are shaped around each number. Then "read" the lines below to fill in and solve each problem.

$$\frac{4 \mid 2}{3 \mid 5}$$

Example:

$$\boxed{4} + \boxed{2} = 6$$

1. ⌐ + ⌐ = ____

2. ⌐ + ⌐ = ____

3. ⌐ + ⌐ = ____

4. ⌐ + ⌐ = ____

5. ⌐ + ⌐ = ____

6. ⌐ + ⌐ = ____

7. ⌐ + ⌐ = ____

8. ⌐ + ⌐ = ____

9. ⌐ + ⌐ = ____

10. ⌐ + ⌐ = ____

Addition & Subtraction Facts to 20 ©2002 Creative Teaching Press

Name _____   Date _____

Mousy Maze

Help the mouse find the cheese! Begin at **Start** and draw a line from the mouse to the cheese. Then go back and solve each problem. Circle the letters next to the sums of 4 or less. Write the circled letters in order on the lines below.

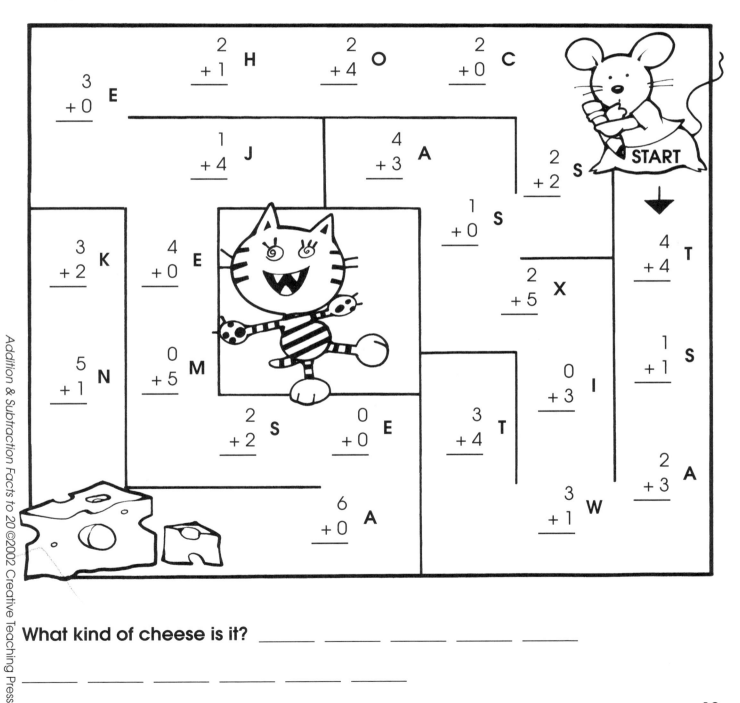

What kind of cheese is it? _____ _____ _____ _____

_____ _____ _____

Name _____ Date _____

Friendship Bracelets

Follow the path from Mia to each friend by subtracting the numbers, starting with 8. Write the final answer on each child's hat.

Mia

8

-1 -3

-3 -0

-3 -2 -1

-2 -1 -2

-1 -2 -1

-2

Addition & Subtraction Facts to 20 ©2002 Creative Teaching Press

Name _____ Date _____

Slay the Dragon

Help the knight slay the dragon! First, draw a line leading the knight to one of the dragons. Then go back to the knight and subtract the numbers along the path, starting with 8. Write your final answer on the dragon's shield.

Name _____ Date _____

Flipping for Sums Game

Materials

coin
score sheet (page 88)
game board (below)
pencils
calculator or counting beans

How to Play

1. **Player A:** Flip a coin onto the game board two times. Add the numbers and write your answer on the score sheet. (If the coin lands off the square, you lose your turn.)

2. **Player B:** Take a turn, flipping the coin and adding your numbers.

3. Take ten turns each. Add all your answers to get your final score, or use a calculator. The player with the *higher* score wins.

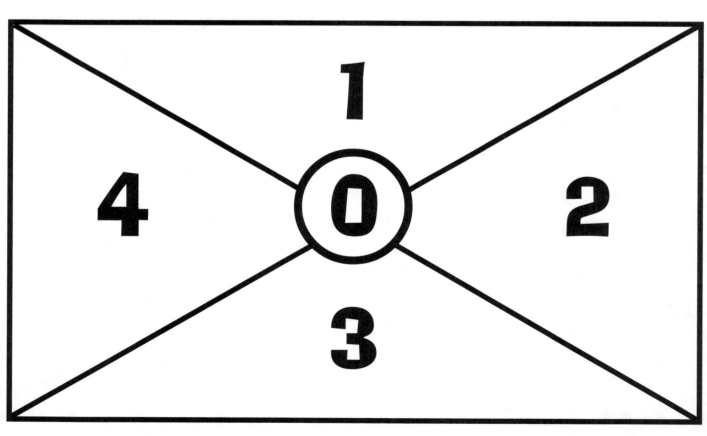

Name _____ Date _____

Calling for Numbers

Add. Then color the correct answer. Write the letters next to the correct answers in order on the lines below. What do you say when you answer the phone?

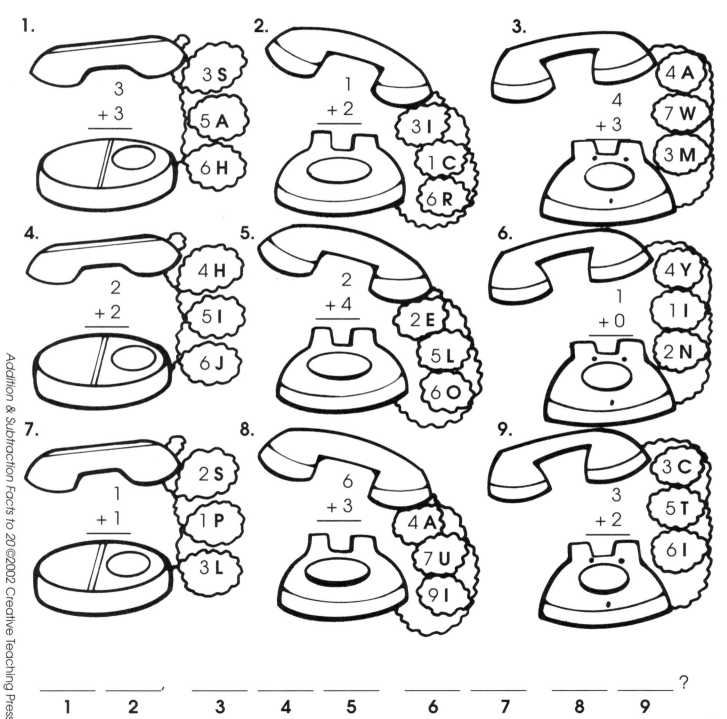

1.
$$\begin{array}{r} 3 \\ + 3 \\ \hline \end{array}$$
3 S
5 A
6 H

2.
$$\begin{array}{r} 1 \\ + 2 \\ \hline \end{array}$$
3 I
1 C
6 R

3.
$$\begin{array}{r} 4 \\ + 3 \\ \hline \end{array}$$
4 A
7 W
3 M

4.
$$\begin{array}{r} 2 \\ + 2 \\ \hline \end{array}$$
4 H
5 I
6 J

5.
$$\begin{array}{r} 2 \\ + 4 \\ \hline \end{array}$$
2 E
5 L
6 O

6.
$$\begin{array}{r} 1 \\ + 0 \\ \hline \end{array}$$
4 Y
1 I
2 N

7.
$$\begin{array}{r} 1 \\ + 1 \\ \hline \end{array}$$
2 S
1 P
3 L

8.
$$\begin{array}{r} 6 \\ + 3 \\ \hline \end{array}$$
4 A
7 U
9 I

9.
$$\begin{array}{r} 3 \\ + 2 \\ \hline \end{array}$$
3 C
5 T
6 I

___ ___ , ___ ___ ___ ___ ___ ___ ___ ?
1   2   3   4   5   6   7   8   9

Name _____ Date _____

Pretty Presents

Add. In each present, circle all the number sentences for the sum on the bow. You should circle 17 sentences in all.

9
4 + 5	1 + 6
5 + 3	2 + 7
6 + 3	2 + 2

8
3 + 3	4 + 4
3 + 5	6 + 3
5 + 2	3 + 4

7
4 + 3	3 + 2
5 + 2	2 + 2
4 + 2	6 + 1

6
2 + 0	1 + 5
3 + 2	4 + 2
3 + 3	3 + 4

5
2 + 2	6 + 3
4 + 1	2 + 3
5 + 0	1 + 6

4

4 + 2
1 + 3
4 + 0

2 + 2
2 + 1
2 + 3

Addition & Subtraction Facts to 20 ©2002 Creative Teaching Press

Name _____ Date _____

Find the Picture

Write the answer for each problem. Then color the picture using the color key.

2 less than 6 _____ **red**

1 less than 9 _____ **yellow**

2 less than 5 _____ **green**

3 less than 8 _____ **blue**

2 less than 9 _____ **purple**

1 less than 7 _____ **orange**

0 less than 9 _____ **brown**

9 less than 9 _____ **black**

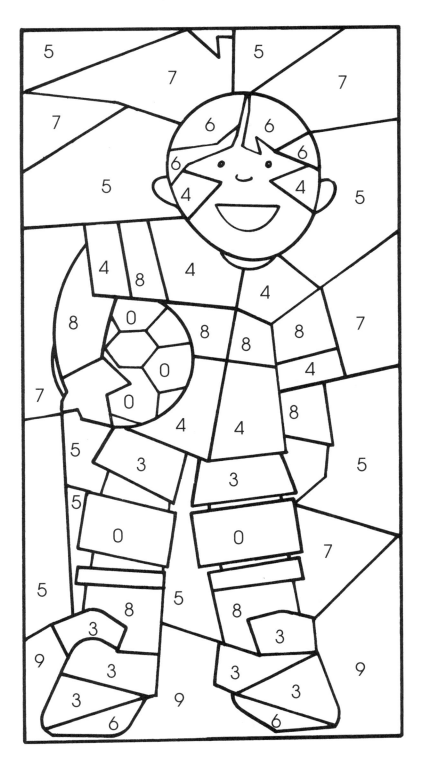

Name _____ Date _____

Under the Umbrella

Find the secret number. The clues will help you. Cross out a number on the umbrella as you read each clue. The number that is left is the secret number.

Clues

1. It is not 8 – 3.

2. It is not 9 – 1.

3. It is not 3 – 3.

4. It is not 8 – 5.

5. It is not 9 – 2.

6. It is not 6 – 4.

7. It is not 9 – 0.

8. It is not 7 – 6.

9. It is not 8 – 2.

Secret number: _____

Name _____ Date _____

Cover the Numbers Game

Materials

deck of cards
pennies or beans
game sheet

How to Play

1. Select the aces, jokers, and number cards 2–9 from a deck of cards. You will have 38 cards. Mix up the cards and place them in a pile, facedown.

   ### Card Values
   Jokers = **0**
   Aces = **1**
   Number cards **2–9** keep their value

2. **Player A:** Draw a card. Use a penny to cover the number you draw, or two pennies to cover two numbers that add up to that number (e.g., if you draw 9, you can cover 9, or 4 and 5, or 6 and 3, etc.).

3. **Player B:** Take a turn, drawing a card and placing pennies.

4. Take turns, until one player covers all of his or her numbers. If you run out of cards, mix them up and use them again.

Player A	Player B
_____	_____
0	0
1	1
2	2
3	3
4	4
5	5
6	6
7	7
8	8
9	9

Addition & Subtraction Facts to 20 ©2002 Creative Teaching Press

Name _____ Date _____

Super Satellite 10

Cut out the number squares at the bottom of the page. Place the numbers in the satellite so that the sum of each row is 10.

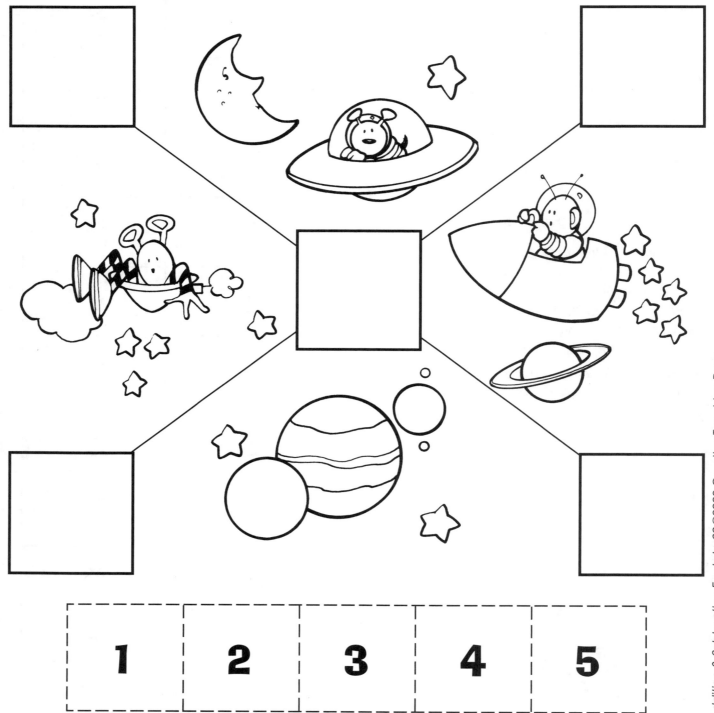

Name _____ Date _____

Puzzle Picture

Add. Then cut out the boxes and glue them in order on another piece of paper. Follow the grid below, from lowest sum to highest sum. If your answers are in the correct order, you will make a picture!

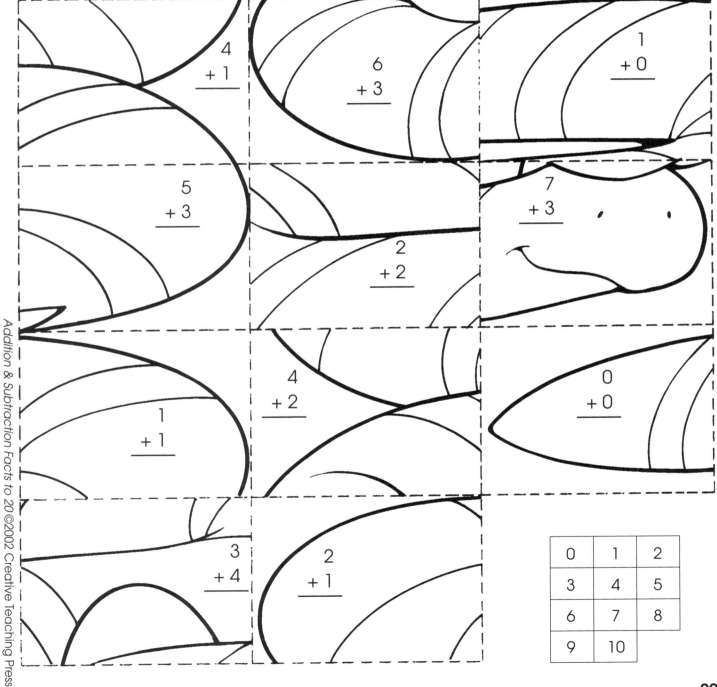

0	1	2
3	4	5
6	7	8
9	10	

Addition & Subtraction Facts to 20 ©2002 Creative Teaching Press

Name _____ Date _____

Secret Code

Subtract. Write the answers in the boxes under the problems. To find the answer to the riddle, write the letters that match the answers on the lines below.

0	1	2	3	4	5	6	7	8	9	10
G	E	T	H	D	I	N	A	V	U	S

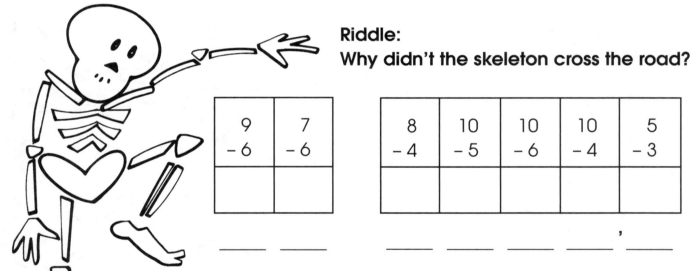

Riddle:
Why didn't the skeleton cross the road?

9	7
− 6	− 6

8	10	10	10	5
− 4	− 5	− 6	− 4	− 3

_____ _____ _____ _____ _____ ,

10	10	8	10
− 7	− 3	− 0	− 9

7	8	2
− 5	− 5	− 1

_____ _____ _____ _____

10	10	6	10
−10	− 1	− 4	− 0

_____ _____ _____ _____ .

Addition & Subtraction Facts to 20 ©2002 Creative Teaching Press

Name _____ Date _____

Half a Sandwich

Subtract. Then match the two sandwich halves with the same answers. Use a crayon to color each match a different color. You will make 9 matches.

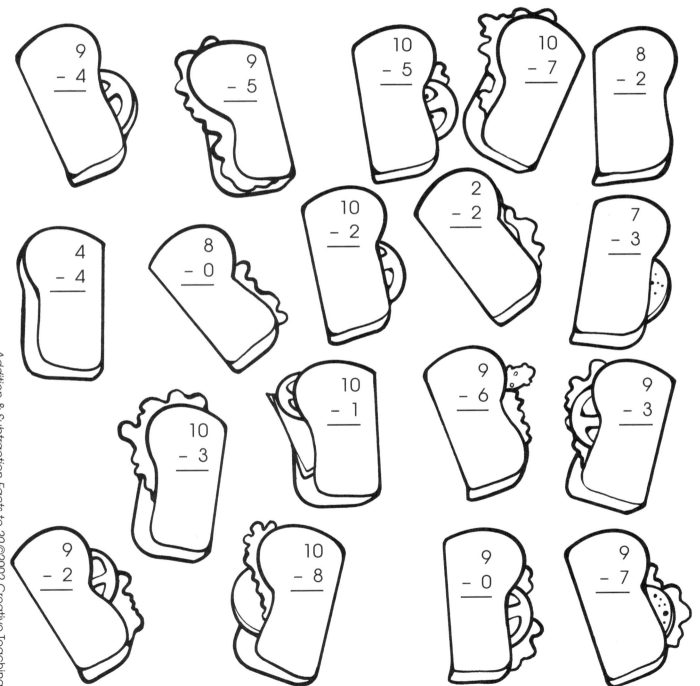

Name _____ Date _____

Soap-Box Derby Game

Materials
20–30 slips of paper or index cards
game board (page 33)
2 game markers
scrap paper
pencils
calculator or counting beans

How to Play
1. Write at least 20 addition and
   subtraction problems on separate slips
   of paper or index cards. Sums and differences can be from 0 to 10. Mix up the cards
   and place them in a pile, facedown.

2. **Player A:** Place a marker on **Start**. Draw a card. Find the answer. If your answer
   is between 0 and 5, move one space. If your answer is between 6 and 10,
   move two spaces. Follow any directions on the board.

3. **Player B:** Take a turn, drawing a card and finding the answer.

4. Take turns. The first person to cross the finish line is the winner.

Addition & Subtraction Facts to 20 ©2002 Creative Teaching Press

Soap-Box Derby Game Board

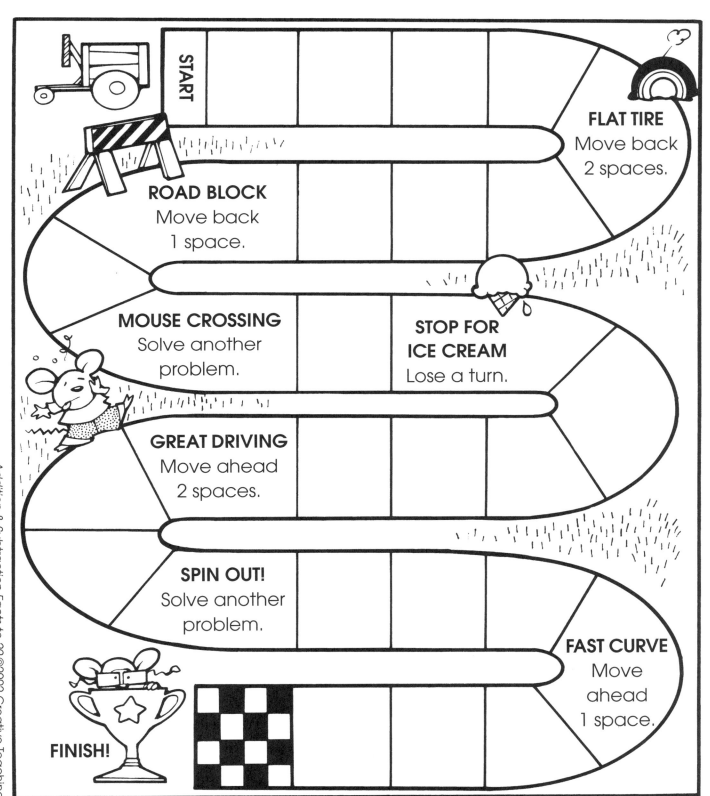

START

FLAT TIRE
Move back
2 spaces.

ROAD BLOCK
Move back
1 space.

MOUSE CROSSING
Solve another
problem.

**STOP FOR
ICE CREAM**
Lose a turn.

GREAT DRIVING
Move ahead
2 spaces.

SPIN OUT!
Solve another
problem.

FAST CURVE
Move
ahead
1 space.

FINISH!

Name _____ Date _____

Bunches of Balloons

Find the secret number. The clues will help you. Cross out a number on a balloon as you read each clue. The number that is left is the secret number.

Clues

1. It is not 5 + 6.

2. It is not 3 + 7.

3. It is not 4 + 4.

4. It is not 2 + 1.

5. It is not 2 + 0.

6. It is not 1 + 4.

7. It is not 7 + 2.

8. It is not 3 + 3.

9. It is not 3 + 1.

4 8 11 3 9 10 5 7 2 6

The secret number is _____.

Name _____ Date _____

Big Splash

There are 12 addition problems in this puzzle. Circle each problem.
They can go across or down.

Hint: A number can be used in more than one problem.

Example:

4	5	3
2	6	8
0	11	1

4	5	9	2	11
6	3	9	3	0
10	3	5	8	11
1	6	5	11	4
11	9	10	2	3

Addition & Subtraction Facts to 20 ©2002 Creative Teaching Press

Name _____ Date _____

Racing Arithmetic

Subtract. Then color the spaces with differences of 6 or less. To solve the riddle, write the letters you colored in order on the lines below.

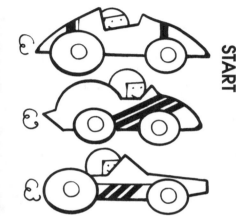

START

| 11
− 5
———
W | 11
− 2
———
A | 10
− 1
———
F | 10
− 7
———
H | 7
− 0
———
B |

| 9
− 8
———
E |

| 11
− 3
———
P | 6
− 4
———
I | 10
− 2
———
Y | 9
− 2
———
G | 7
− 4
———
L | 8
− 3
———
E | 8
− 1
———
K |

| 5
− 2
———
E |

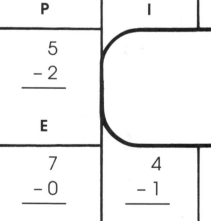

FINISH!

| 7
− 0
———
K | 4
− 1
———
C | 11
− 4
———
N | 11
− 7
———
O | 10
− 3
———
M | 10
− 5
———
O | 11
− 8
———
L |

Riddle: What did the racecar think of the new track?

He thought it was _____ _____ _____ _____ _____ _____ _____

_____ _____ _____ _____!

Addition & Subtraction Facts to 20 ©2002 Creative Teaching Press

Name _____ Date _____

Clowning Around

Subtract. Then color the circus scene using the answers in the color key. Use any color for spaces without numbers.

0, 1 = **red**   2, 3 = **yellow**   4, 5 = **green**
6, 7 = **blue**   8, 9 = **purple**   10, 11 = **orange**

Name _____ Date _____

Trick-Tac-Toe Game

Materials

20–30 slips of paper or index cards
game sheet
pencils

How to Play

1. Write at least 20 addition and subtraction problems on separate slips of paper or index cards. Sums and differences can be from 0 to 11. Mix up the cards and place them in a pile, facedown.

2. **Player A:** Draw a card. Find the answer. If the answer is between 0 and 6, mark an X on a Trick-Tac-Toe grid. If the answer is between 7 and 11, skip your turn.

3. **Player B:** Take a turn. If the answer is between 7 and 11, mark an O on the grid. If the answer is between 0 and 6, skip your turn.

4. Take turns until a player gets three Xs or Os in a row, across, down, or diagonally. Play at least six games.

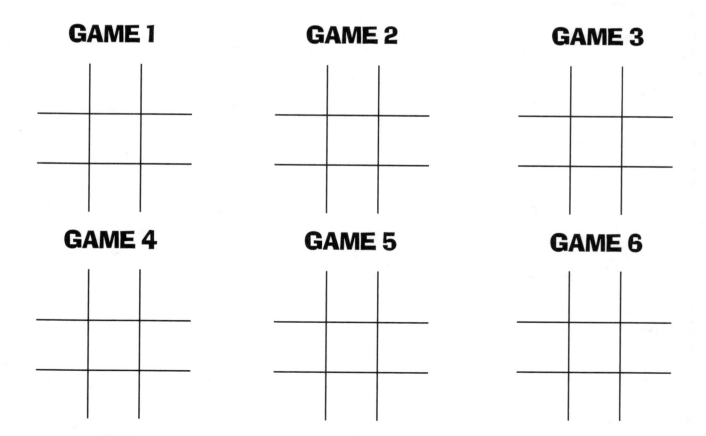

GAME 1   **GAME 2**   **GAME 3**

GAME 4   **GAME 5**   **GAME 6**

Addition & Subtraction Facts to 20 ©2002 Creative Teaching Press

Name _____ Date _____

Six-Square Stumpers

Look at the number puzzle and see how the lines are shaped around each number. Then "read" the lines below to fill in and solve each problem.

$$
\begin{array}{c|c|c}
1 & 2 & 3 \\
\hline
4 & 5 & 6
\end{array}
$$

Example:

$$\boxed{6} \ + \ \ulcorner 3 \ = 9$$

1. ⌐ + ⌐ = _____

2. ⌈ + ⌊ = _____

3. ⌈⌉ + ⌊⌋ = _____

4. ⌊ + ⌐ = _____

5. ⌐ + ⌐ = _____

6. ⌈ + ⌊ = _____

7. ⌈⌉ + ⌈⌉ = _____

8. ⌈ + ⌈ = _____

9. ⌈⌉ + ⌈ = _____

10. ⌊⌋ + ⌐ = _____

11. ⌈⌉ + ⌈⌉ = _____

12. ⌈⌉ + ⌊ = _____

Name _____ Date _____

Milo Martian's Mile

Add. Then mark Milo Martian's path by coloring all the footprints that have the sum of 12.

Name _____ Date _____

Color Me Pretty

Subtract. Then color each part that has an answer between 6 and 12.

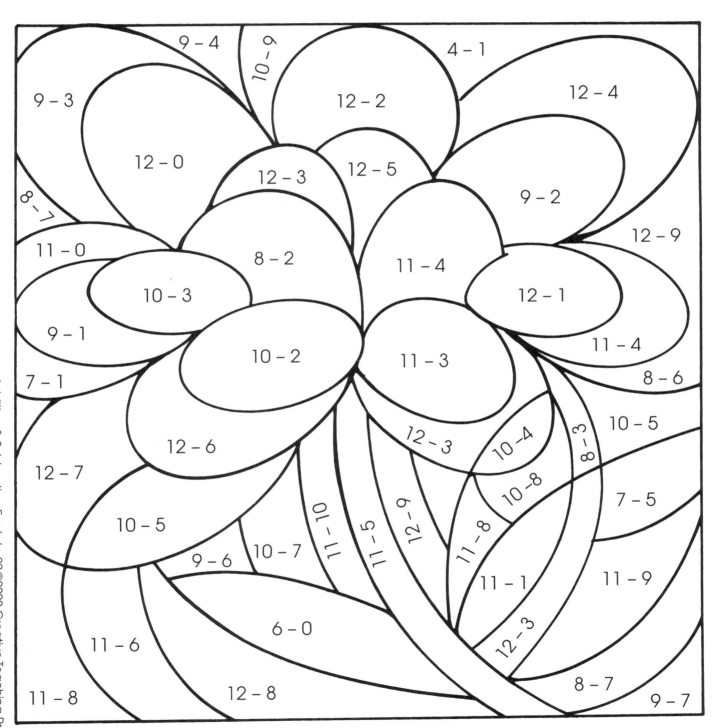

Name _____ Date _____

Super 12 Square

There are 13 subtraction problems in this puzzle. Circle each problem.
They can go across or down.

Hint: A number can be used in more than one problem.

Example:

12	1	11	7	4
8	0	12	6	6
4	6	4	1	6
4	4	8	5	3
12	2	10	7	3

Addition & Subtraction Facts to 20 ©2002 Creative Teaching Press

Name _____ Date _____

On a Roll Game

Materials

2 dice
score sheet (page 88)
pencils
calculator or counting beans

How to Play

1. **Player A:** Roll the dice and add the number of dots shown. Write your answer on the score sheet.

2. **Player B:** Take a turn, rolling the dice and adding the dots. Write your answer on the score sheet.

3. Take ten turns each. Add all your answers to get your score, or use a calculator. The player with the *higher* score wins.

$3+1=4$

Name _____ Date _____

Pigs on the Go!

Write the missing number for each set of addition sentences.

T	I	S	N	P
6 + ___ = 13	___ + 9 = 13	8 + ___ = 13	10 + ___ = 13	7 + ___ = 13
___ + 6 = 13	9 + ___ = 13	___ + 8 = 13	___ + 10 = 13	___ + 7 = 13
G	**U**	**C**	**R**	**K**
5 + ___ = 13	4 + ___ = 13	3 + ___ = 13	11 + ___ = 13	12 + ___ = 13
___ + 5 = 13	___ + 4 = 13	___ + 3 = 13	___ + 11 = 13	___ + 12 = 13

To solve the riddle, write the letters that match the numbers on the lines below.

Riddle: How do pigs travel?

___ ___   ___ ___ ___ ___ - ___
 4   3   6   4   8   9   6

___ ___ ___ ___ ___
 7   2   9 10   1   5

Addition & Subtraction Facts to 20 ©2002 Creative Teaching Press

Name _____ Date _____

Weight and See

Find each sum. Then color the bigger sum in each pair. Write the colored letters in order on the lines below.

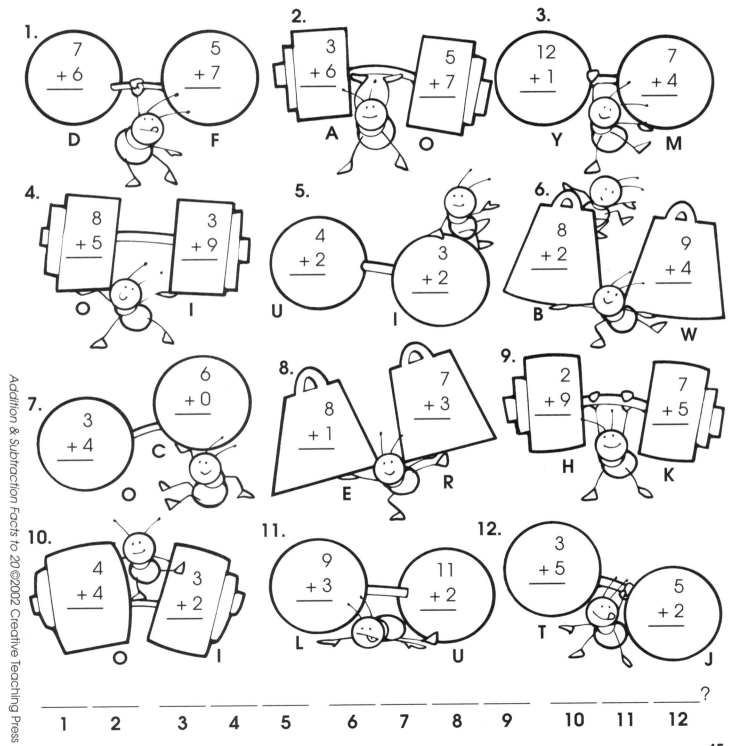

1.

$\begin{array}{r} 7 \\ +6 \\ \hline \end{array}$ D

$\begin{array}{r} 5 \\ +7 \\ \hline \end{array}$ F

2.

$\begin{array}{r} 3 \\ +6 \\ \hline \end{array}$ A

$\begin{array}{r} 5 \\ +7 \\ \hline \end{array}$ O

3.

$\begin{array}{r} 12 \\ +1 \\ \hline \end{array}$ Y

$\begin{array}{r} 7 \\ +4 \\ \hline \end{array}$ M

4.

$\begin{array}{r} 8 \\ +5 \\ \hline \end{array}$ O

$\begin{array}{r} 3 \\ +9 \\ \hline \end{array}$ I

5.

$\begin{array}{r} 4 \\ +2 \\ \hline \end{array}$ U

$\begin{array}{r} 3 \\ +2 \\ \hline \end{array}$ I

6.

$\begin{array}{r} 8 \\ +2 \\ \hline \end{array}$ B

$\begin{array}{r} 9 \\ +4 \\ \hline \end{array}$ W

7.

$\begin{array}{r} 3 \\ +4 \\ \hline \end{array}$ O

$\begin{array}{r} 6 \\ +0 \\ \hline \end{array}$ C

8.

$\begin{array}{r} 8 \\ +1 \\ \hline \end{array}$ E

$\begin{array}{r} 7 \\ +3 \\ \hline \end{array}$ R

9.

$\begin{array}{r} 2 \\ +9 \\ \hline \end{array}$ H

$\begin{array}{r} 7 \\ +5 \\ \hline \end{array}$ K

10.

$\begin{array}{r} 4 \\ +4 \\ \hline \end{array}$ O

$\begin{array}{r} 3 \\ +2 \\ \hline \end{array}$ I

11.

$\begin{array}{r} 9 \\ +3 \\ \hline \end{array}$ L

$\begin{array}{r} 11 \\ +2 \\ \hline \end{array}$ U

12.

$\begin{array}{r} 3 \\ +5 \\ \hline \end{array}$ T

$\begin{array}{r} 5 \\ +2 \\ \hline \end{array}$ J

___ ___ ___ ___ ___ ___ ___ ___ ___ ___ ___ ___ ?
 1   2   3   4   5   6   7   8   9   10 11 12

Name _____ Date _____

Mitten Match

Use a crayon to follow each string and match each pair of mittens.
Write the answer for each subtraction problem on the matching mitten.

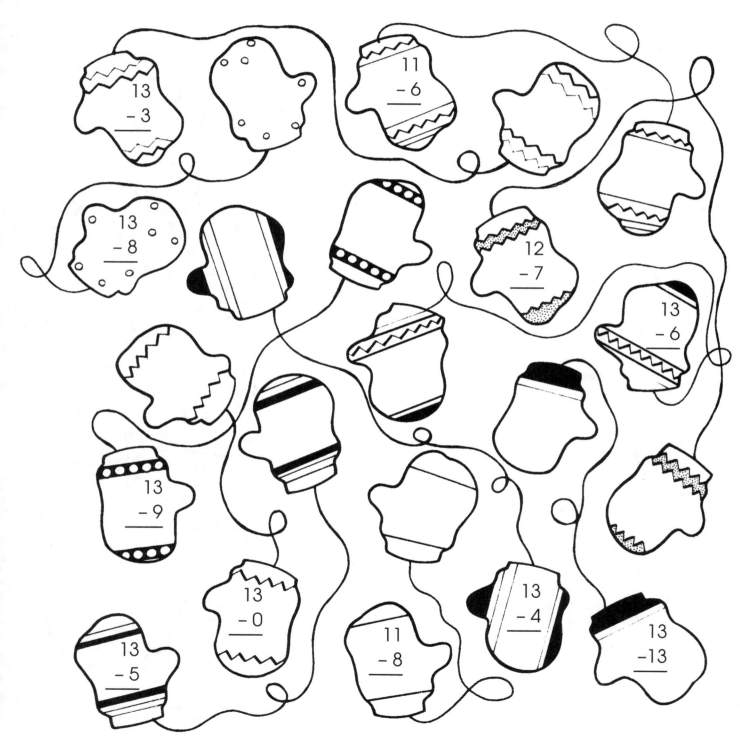

Name _____ Date _____

Something Fishy

Help the shark catch the fish! Follow the path from the shark to each fish, subtracting the numbers from 13. Write your final answer on the fish.

Name _____ Date _____

Map Math Game

Materials

game cards (page 49)
scissors
scrap paper
pencils
score sheet (page 88)
calculator or counting beans

How to Play

1. Cut out the game cards. Mix up the cards and place them in a pile, facedown.

2. **Player A:** Draw a card. Find the two towns on the map and add the numbers. (Cards with stars are "challenge" problems. The correct answer earns one extra point.) Write the sum as your score.

3. **Player B:** Take a turn and record your sum.

4. Take turns, until all cards are gone. Add up each player's answers, or use a calculator. The player with the *higher* score wins.

5. Then mix up the cards and play again. This time, subtract the smaller number from the larger number. The player with the *lower* score wins.

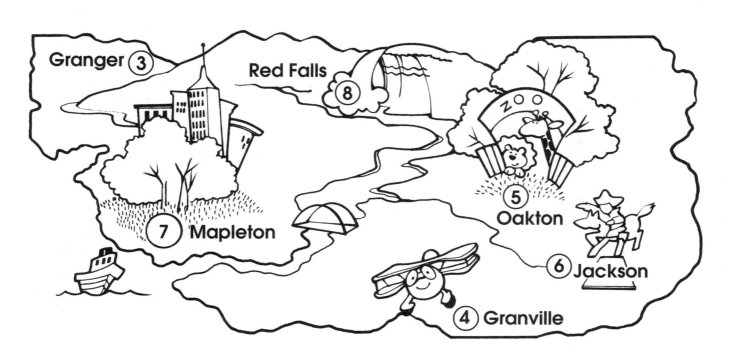

Addition & Subtraction Facts to 20 ©2002 Creative Teaching Press

Map Math Game Cards

Oakton to Granville	**Red Falls to Granger**
Granger to Granville	**Jackson to Mapleton**
Granger to Jackson	**Oakton to Jackson**
Oakton to Mapleton	**Granville to Red Falls**
Mapleton to Granger	**Jackson to Red Falls** ★
Oakton to Red Falls	**Granville to Jackson**
Granger to Oakton	**Mapleton to Granville**
Red Falls to Mapleton ★	**1 BONUS POINT**

Name _____ Date _____

Magic Squares

Add the numbers across. Then add the numbers down. Write the sums in the triangles. If the sums are correct, the numbers in the triangles will add up to the same sum. Write your final answer in the circle.

Example:

+	2	3	▽ **5**
	4	3	▽ **7**
	▷ **6**	▷ **6**	◯ **12**

+	3	4	▽
	2	5	▽
	▷	▷	◯

+	0	4	▽
	5	4	▽
	▷	▷	◯

+	2	2	▽
	4	3	▽
	▷	▷	◯

+	5	1	▽
	4	2	▽
	▷	▷	◯

+	4	0	▽
	2	5	▽
	▷	▷	◯

+	3	1	▽
	6	2	▽
	▷	▷	◯

+	1	5	▽
	3	4	▽
	▷	▷	◯

+	3	5	▽
	3	2	▽
	▷	▷	◯

Addition & Subtraction Facts to 20 ©2002 Creative Teaching Press

Name _____ Date _____

Bulls-Eye!

Look at the number in the middle of each target. Then write the number, that when added to the middle number, equals the sum on the outside of the target. The first one is done for you.

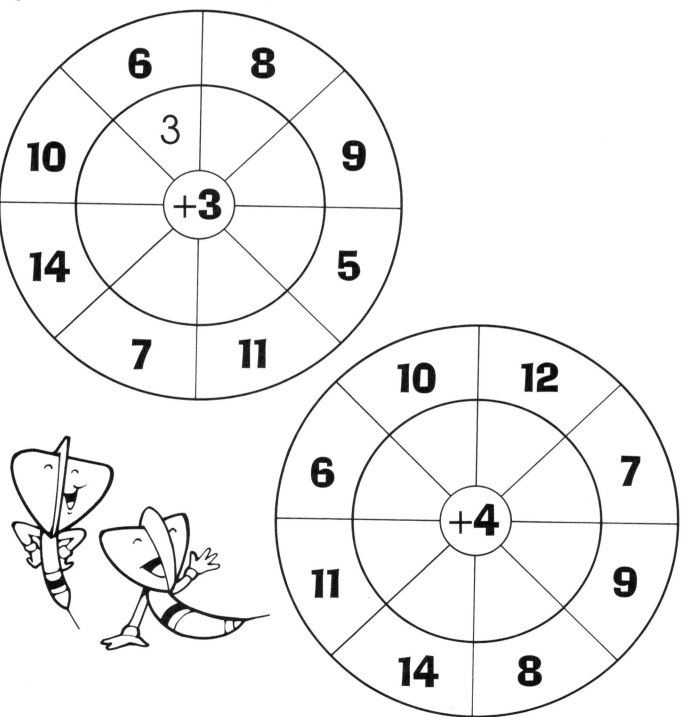

Name _____ Date _____

Dot-to-Dot Zoo

Subtract. Then use a crayon to follow the dots in the order of your answers, from 1 to 14.

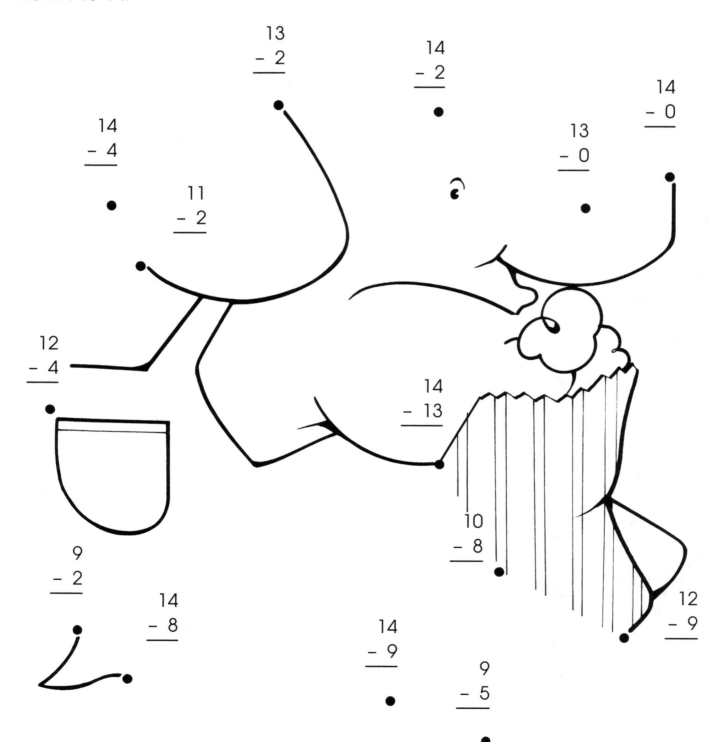

Addition & Subtraction Facts to 20 ©2002 Creative Teaching Press

Name _____ Date _____

Cross It Out

Subtract. For each answer, place an X on each player's card that has that number. The player with five Xs wins.

Silly Squirrel

5	13	10
1	11	7

Rowdy Rabbit

6	14	8
10	4	12

$$\begin{array}{r} 14 \\ -\ 9 \\ \hline \end{array} \qquad \begin{array}{r} 13 \\ -\ 7 \\ \hline \end{array} \qquad \begin{array}{r} 12 \\ -\ 9 \\ \hline \end{array} \qquad \begin{array}{r} 14 \\ -\ 0 \\ \hline \end{array}$$

$$\begin{array}{r} 12 \\ -\ 4 \\ \hline \end{array} \qquad \begin{array}{r} 13 \\ -\ 4 \\ \hline \end{array} \qquad \begin{array}{r} 11 \\ -\ 1 \\ \hline \end{array} \qquad \begin{array}{r} 14 \\ -\ 7 \\ \hline \end{array}$$

$$\begin{array}{r} 4 \\ -\ 2 \\ \hline \end{array} \qquad \begin{array}{r} 12 \\ -\ 11 \\ \hline \end{array} \qquad \begin{array}{r} 9 \\ -\ 9 \\ \hline \end{array} \qquad \begin{array}{r} 13 \\ -\ 2 \\ \hline \end{array}$$

Who wins the game? _____

Name _____ Date _____

Perfect Pairs Game

Materials
deck of cards
score sheet (page 88)
pencils
calculator or counting beans

How to Play

1. Select the jokers, aces, and number cards 2–7 from a deck of cards. You will have 30 cards. Mix up the cards and place them in a pile, facedown.

   ### Card Values
   Jokers = **0**
   Aces = **1**
   Number cards **2–7** keep their value

2. **Player A:** Draw two cards. Add the numbers on your cards by writing a number sentence on the score sheet. Return the cards to the bottom of the pile.

3. **Player B:** Take a turn and record your number sentence.

4. Take 10 turns each. Add all your answers to get your score, or use a calculator. The player with the *higher* score wins.

Addition & Subtraction Facts to 20 ©2002 Creative Teaching Press

Name _____   Date _____

Sneaky Snakes

How many snakes can you find in the picture? Complete the puzzle to find the answer. Then find and circle that number of snakes.

1	+ 3	+ 6	+ 3 =	**Answer:**

On the back of this paper, write the answer. Then write 14 number sentences that add up to that sum.

Name _____ Date _____

Brick by Brick

Add. Then help Sally Spider climb the wall. Color the bricks that have the sum of 15 to show Sally how to get back to her web.

HOME!

| 3 + 9 = | 6 + 2 = | 9 + 6 = | 11 + 4 = |

| 4 + 7 = | 14 + 1 = | 3 + 9 = | 8 + 2 = |

| 7 + 4 = | 10 + 5 = | 8 + 7 = | 8 + 5 = |

| 9 + 4 = | 9 + 5 = | 15 + 0 = | 9 + 1 = |

| 7 + 7 = | 6 + 6 = | 2 + 12 = | 3 + 12 = |

| 3 + 9 = | 10 + 4 = | 6 + 9 = |

| 7 + 5 = | 4 + 8 = | 11 + 2 = | 12 + 3 = |

| 3 + 6 = | 4 + 5 = | 11 + 4 = |

| 6 + 6 = | 7 + 8 = | 6 + 9 = | 7 + 6 = |

START

Addition & Subtraction Facts to 20 ©2002 Creative Teaching Press

Name _____ Date _____

Letter Search

Color the problem in each row that has the answer on the left.
If your answers are correct, you will form a letter.

12	15 – 3	15 – 1	10 – 2	14 – 3	13 – 1
9	15 – 7	15 – 6	12 – 8	13 – 4	14 – 7
6	12 – 5	10 – 5	15 – 9	12 – 7	13 – 8
8	11 – 5	12 – 4	10 – 1	8 – 0	14 – 9
4	13 – 9	12 – 6	11 – 4	9 – 4	10 – 6

Addition & Subtraction Facts to 20 ©2002 Creative Teaching Press

What letter did you make? _____

Name _____ Date _____

Changing Butterflies

Use a pencil to draw a line from a caterpillar to a chrysalis to a butterfly to make a subtraction sentence.

Hint: You can use each number only once.

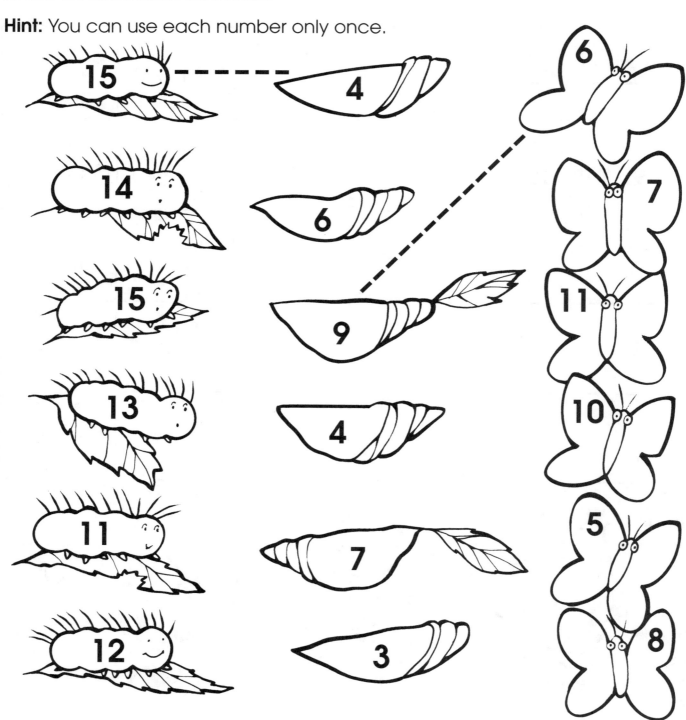

Name _____ Date _____

Sum Find 1 Game

8	10
13	15

Materials
score sheet (page 88)
pencils

How to Play

1. **Player A:** Choose a sum from the grid above. Then find two numbers below connected by a line that equal that sum. Write the addition sentence on the score sheet.

2. **Player B:** Find two more numbers that equal that sum. Write the addition sentence.

3. Take turns until you find all the addition sentences that equal that sum. Player B then picks a new sum from the grid. Take turns finding and writing addition sentences. You will find 13 total.

Note: 3 + 5 and 5 + 3 count as one addition sentence.

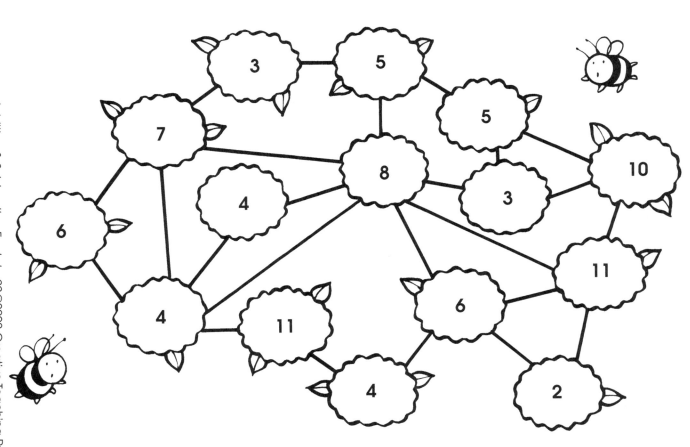

Name _____ Date _____

Sum Find 2 Game

15	12
14	11

Materials
score sheet (page 88)
pencils

How to Play

1. **Player A:** Choose a sum from the grid above. This time you can connect two or three numbers to get each sum. You will find 21 total number sentences. Write the number sentence on the score sheet.

2. **Player B:** Find two more numbers that equal that sum. Write the number sentence.

3. Take turns until you find all the number sentences that equal that sum. Player B then picks a new sum from the grid. Take turns finding and writing number sentences. You will find 21 total.

Hint: 3 + 8 and 8 + 3 count as one sentence in this activity.

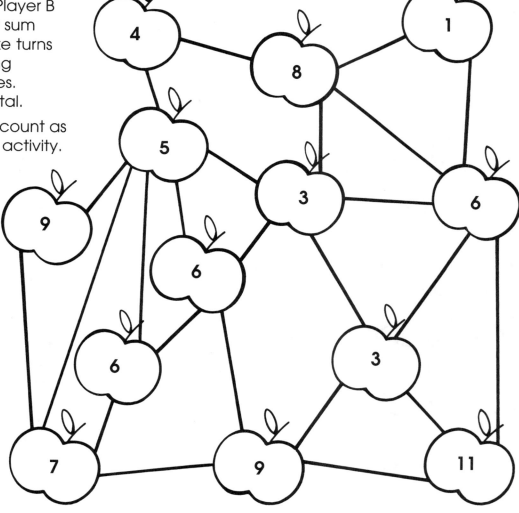

Name _____ Date _____

On Target

Look at the number in the middle of the target. in each space write the number, that when added to 5, equals the sum on the outside of the target. Then color the target—odd numbers **red** and even numbers **blue**.

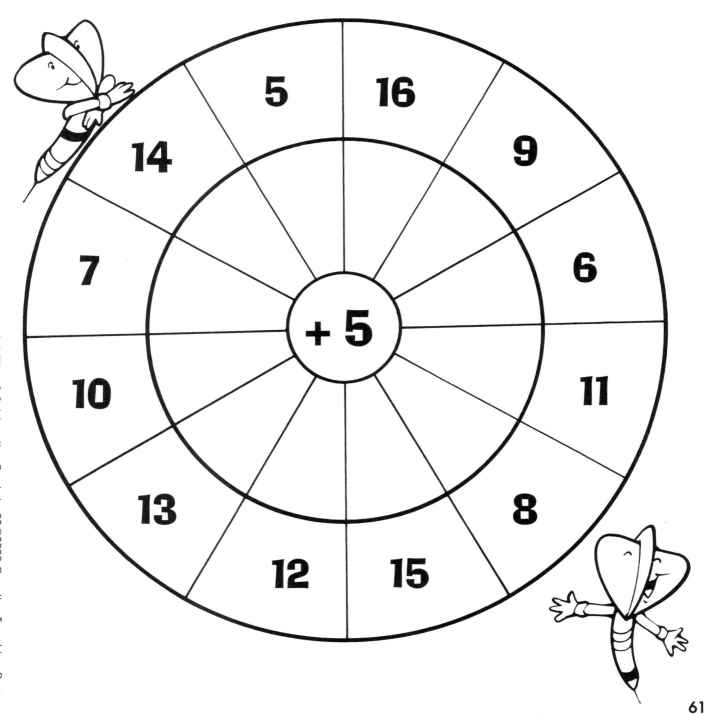

Name _____ Date _____

Apple Match

Add. Then match the apple halves with the same sums. Use a crayon to color each match a different color. You will make 10 matches.

Addition & Subtraction Facts to 20 ©2002 Creative Teaching Press

Name _____ Date _____

Under the Sea

Subtract. Then color the underwater scene using the differences in the color key. Use any color for spaces without numbers.

0 to 2 = **green**   5 to 7 = **blue**   11 to 13 = **yellow**

3 to 4 = **red**   8 to 10 = **purple**   14 to 16 = **pink**

Name _____ Date _____

Number Scramble 16

Choose two numbers in each group to make subtraction sentences. Cross out the two numbers in each group that you did not use.

Example:

9 ~~5~~ 7 ~~4~~

16 - __9__ = __7__

16 - __7__ = __9__

---

6   4   9   8

15 - _____ = _____

15 - _____ = _____

---

3   6   4   9

10 - _____ = _____

10 - _____ = _____

---

6   4   8   5

12 - _____ = _____

12 - _____ = _____

---

3   6   8   5

13 - _____ = _____

13 - _____ = _____

---

8   4   7   9

16 - _____ = _____

16 - _____ = _____

---

6   9   2   8

14 - _____ = _____

14 - _____ = _____

---

5   8   6   7

11 - _____ = _____

11 - _____ = _____

---

3   6   2   5

9 - _____ = _____

9 - _____ = _____

---

4   8   8   7

16 - _____ = _____

16 - _____ = _____

---

2   3   4   6

8 - _____ = _____

8 - _____ = _____

---

6   7   4   8

15 - _____ = _____

15 - _____ = _____

Addition & Subtraction Facts to 20 ©2002 Creative Teaching Press

Name _____ Date _____

Take a Spin Game

Materials

tagboard
glue, scissors
crayons, pencils
hole punch
brass fastener
score sheet (page 88)
calculator or counting beans

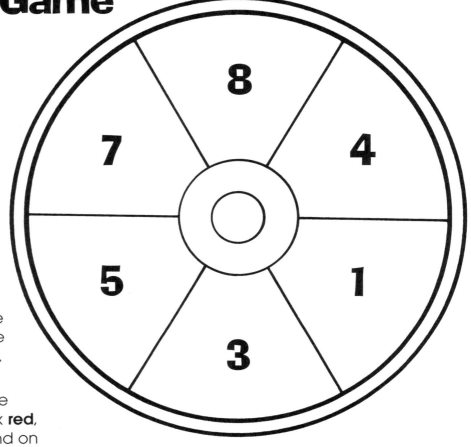

How to Play

1. Glue the wheel and spinner to tagboard and cut them out. Color the spinner, punch a hole in the middle, and attach it to the wheel with a brass fastener. (See the example below.)

2. **Player A:** Pick a color on the spinner and spin. If you pick **red**, double the number you land on (e.g., if you land on 5, add 5 + 5). If you pick **blue**, add the numbers across from each other (e.g., if you land on 5, add 5 + 4).

3. **Player B:** Take a turn and add the numbers.

4. Take 10 turns each. Add all your answers to get your score, or use a calculator. The player with the *higher* score wins.

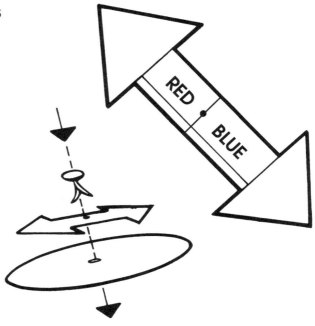

Spider Web

Cut out the number squares at the bottom of the page. Place the numbers in the spider web so that the sum of each row is 17. One number will be left over. What is it? _____

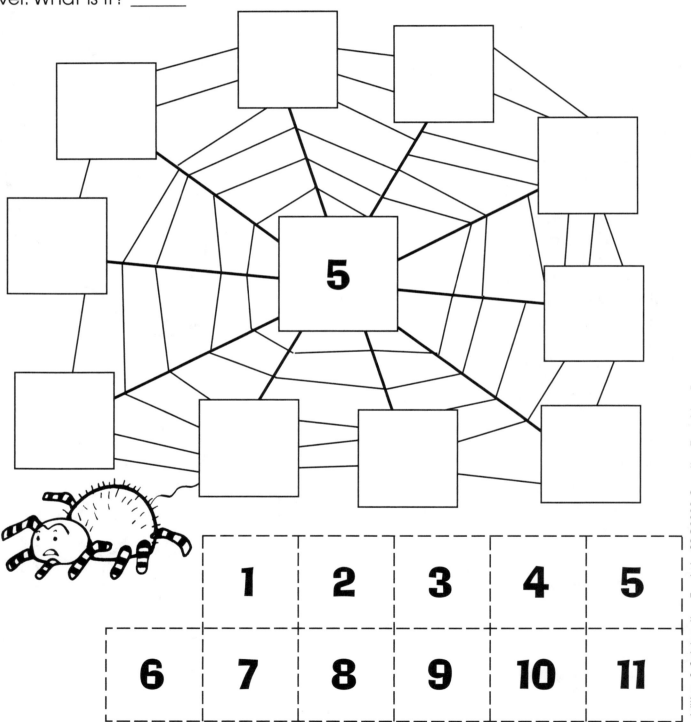

Name _____ Date _____

Line Puzzle

Look at the number puzzle and see how the lines are shaped around each number. Then "read" the lines below to fill in and solve each problem.

$$10 \mid 6 \mid 4 . \mid 7$$
$$\overline{5 \mid 9 \mid 3 . \mid 8}$$

Example:

$$\boxed{8} + \boxed{9} = 17$$

1. ___ + ___ = _____

2. ___ + ___ = _____

3. ___ + ___ = _____

4. ___ + ___ = _____

5. ___ + ___ = _____

6. ___ + ___ = _____

7. ___ + ___ = _____

8. ___ + ___ = _____

9. ___ + ___ = _____

10. ___ + ___ = _____

11. ___ + ___ = _____

12. ___ + ___ = _____

Name _____ Date _____

Play Ball!

Subtract. Then color the spaces with answers of 8 or less. Starting at the arrow, write the letters you colored in order on the lines below. If your answers are correct, you'll solve the riddle!

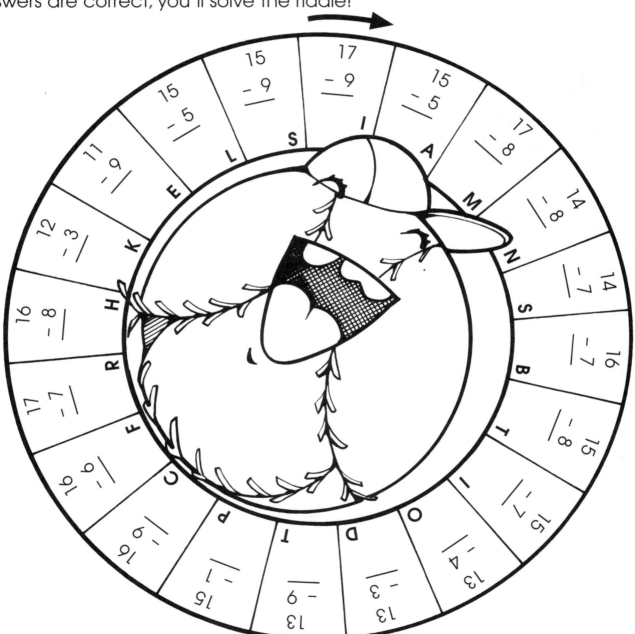

Riddle: How did the player know the baseball was laughing?

Answer: It was _____ _____ _____ _____ _____ _____ _____ _____ _____ _____.

Name _____ Date _____

Balloon Pop!

Subtract. Then follow the strings to see which two balloons are connected. "Pop" the balloon with the lower answer in each pair by drawing an X over it.

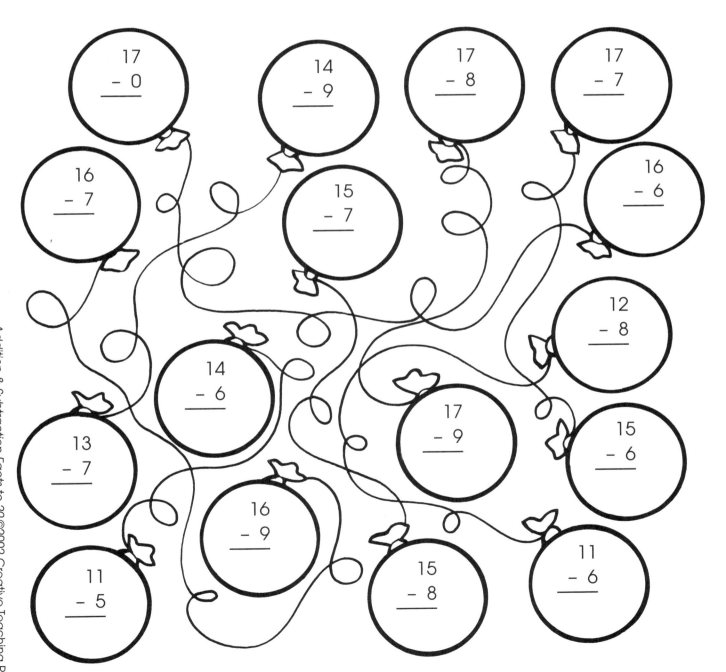

Name _____ Date _____

"O" My! Game

Materials
scissors
game squares (pages 70 and 71)

How to Play

1. Cut out the squares. Place the square with the face on the table.

2. **Player A:** Place the side of a square with an addition problem next to another square with the correct sum. Place the problem and sum directly next to each other.

3. **Player B:** Take a turn, matching an addition problem to its sum.

4. Take turns until you make a letter.

What letter did you make? _____

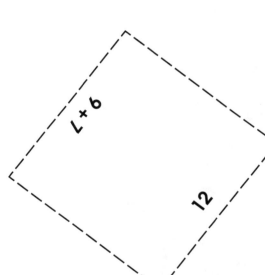

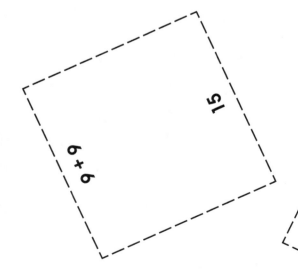

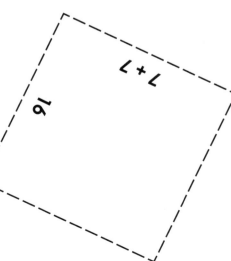

Addition & Subtraction Facts to 20 ©2002 Creative Teaching Press

"O" My! Game

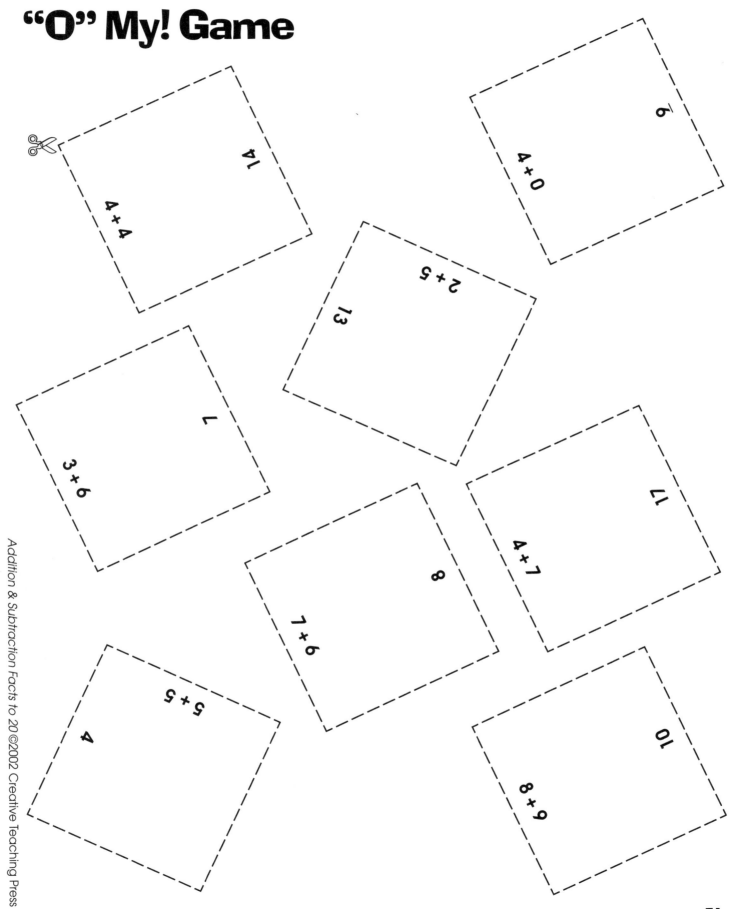

Name _____ Date _____

Shifty Shapes

Add the numbers across. Then add the numbers down. Write the sums in the triangles. If the sums are correct, the numbers in the triangles will add up to the same sum. Write your final answer in the circle.

+ 3 6 / 4 5	+ 5 3 / 1 6	+ 1 4 / 8 3
+ 2 5 / 2 4	+ 8 4 / 1 5	+ 3 5 / 4 0
+ 3 5 / 1 6	+ 4 8 / 2 3	+ 5 2 / 6 4

Name _____ Date _____

Hungry Hippo

Add. Then color the correct answer. To solve the puzzle, write the letters next to the answers in order on the lines below.

1.

8
+ 8
____

15   **B**
16   **C**
12   **M**

2.

7
+ 4
____

12   **G**
9   **W**
11   **H**

3.

4
+ 5
____

9   **O**
6   **L**
8   **H**

4.

5
+ 8
____

11   **E**
13   **C**
12   **T**

5.

9
+ 9
____

18   **O**
12   **U**
16   **D**

6.

10
+ 8
____

16   **V**
17   **K**
18   **L**

7.

9
+ 8
____

12   **I**
15   **O**
17   **A**

8.

8
+ 7
____

15   **T**
13   **Q**
17   **S**

9.

6
+ 6
____

15   **A**
12   **E**
11   **T**

What kind of sundae did Hungry Hippo order?

____ ____ ____ ____ ____ ____ ____ ____ ____
 1   2   3   4   5   6   7   8   9

Name _____ Date _____

Towering Castles

In each tower, circle all the number sentences that equal the sum on the roof. What sum is in the tower with the most circled sentences? _____

6

15 – 9
16 – 6
12 – 6
9 – 5
7 – 1
13 – 7

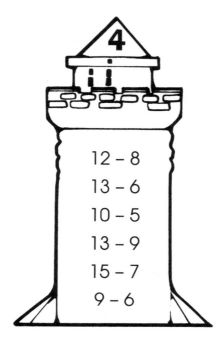

4

12 – 8
13 – 6
10 – 5
13 – 9
15 – 7
9 – 6

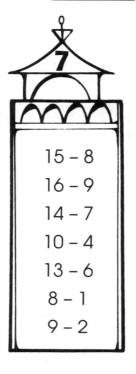

7

15 – 8
16 – 9
14 – 7
10 – 4
13 – 6
8 – 1
9 – 2

5

12 – 6
13 – 8
12 – 7
7 – 4
10 – 5
9 – 2
8 – 6
11 – 7

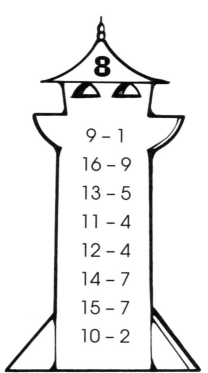

8

9 – 1
16 – 9
13 – 5
11 – 4
12 – 4
14 – 7
15 – 7
10 – 2

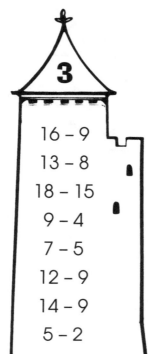

3

16 – 9
13 – 8
18 – 15
9 – 4
7 – 5
12 – 9
14 – 9
5 – 2

Name _____ Date _____

Take a Hike

Follow each path, subtracting as you go to find the final answer. Write the answer on the line. Then circle the house with the smallest number.

Addition & Subtraction Facts to 20 ©2002 Creative Teaching Press

Name _____ Date _____

Triple Roll Game

Materials
3 dice
score sheet (below)
pencils
calculator or counting beans

= 10

How to Play

1. **Player A:** Roll the dice and add all the dots shown. (See the example above.) Write your addition sentence on the score sheet.

2. **Player B:** Take a turn, rolling the dice and writing the addition sentence.

3. Take eight turns each. Add all your answers to get your score, or use a calculator. The player with the *higher* score wins.

Score Sheet

Player A _____	Player B _____
1. ____ + ____ + ____ = ____	1. ____ + ____ + ____ = ____
2. ____ + ____ + ____ = ____	2. ____ + ____ + ____ = ____
3. ____ + ____ + ____ = ____	3. ____ + ____ + ____ = ____
4. ____ + ____ + ____ = ____	4. ____ + ____ + ____ = ____
5. ____ + ____ + ____ = ____	5. ____ + ____ + ____ = ____
6. ____ + ____ + ____ = ____	6. ____ + ____ + ____ = ____
7. ____ + ____ + ____ = ____	7. ____ + ____ + ____ = ____
8. ____ + ____ + ____ = ____	8. ____ + ____ + ____ = ____
Score: ____	Score: ____

Addition & Subtraction Facts to 20 ©2002 Creative Teaching Press

Name _____   Date _____

Drawing with Dots

Add. Then use a crayon to connect the dots in the order of your answers, from 0 to 19.

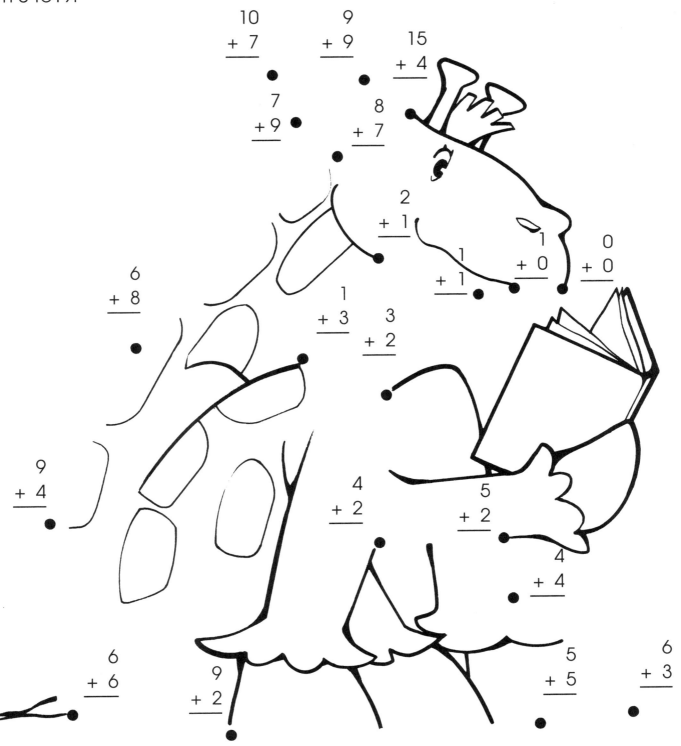

$$\begin{array}{r} 10 \\ + 7 \\ \hline \end{array}$$
$$\begin{array}{r} 9 \\ + 9 \\ \hline \end{array}$$
$$\begin{array}{r} 15 \\ + 4 \\ \hline \end{array}$$
$$\begin{array}{r} 7 \\ + 9 \\ \hline \end{array}$$
$$\begin{array}{r} 8 \\ + 7 \\ \hline \end{array}$$
$$\begin{array}{r} 2 \\ + 1 \\ \hline \end{array}$$
$$\begin{array}{r} 1 \\ + 0 \\ \hline \end{array}$$
$$\begin{array}{r} 0 \\ + 0 \\ \hline \end{array}$$
$$\begin{array}{r} 1 \\ + 1 \\ \hline \end{array}$$
$$\begin{array}{r} 6 \\ + 8 \\ \hline \end{array}$$
$$\begin{array}{r} 1 \\ + 3 \\ \hline \end{array}$$
$$\begin{array}{r} 3 \\ + 2 \\ \hline \end{array}$$
$$\begin{array}{r} 9 \\ + 4 \\ \hline \end{array}$$
$$\begin{array}{r} 4 \\ + 2 \\ \hline \end{array}$$
$$\begin{array}{r} 5 \\ + 2 \\ \hline \end{array}$$
$$\begin{array}{r} 4 \\ + 4 \\ \hline \end{array}$$
$$\begin{array}{r} 6 \\ + 6 \\ \hline \end{array}$$
$$\begin{array}{r} 9 \\ + 2 \\ \hline \end{array}$$
$$\begin{array}{r} 5 \\ + 5 \\ \hline \end{array}$$
$$\begin{array}{r} 6 \\ + 3 \\ \hline \end{array}$$

Name _____ Date _____

Lucky Ladybug

Find the ladybug's lucky number. The clues will help you. Cross out a number on the ladybug as you read each clue. The number that is left is the lucky number.

Clues

1. It is not 7 + 5.

2. It is not 13 + 6.

3. It is not 7 + 4.

4. It is not 9 + 9.

5. It is not 5 + 8.

6. It is not 9 + 8.

7. It is not 6 + 4.

8. It is not 6 + 9.

9. It is not 7 + 7.

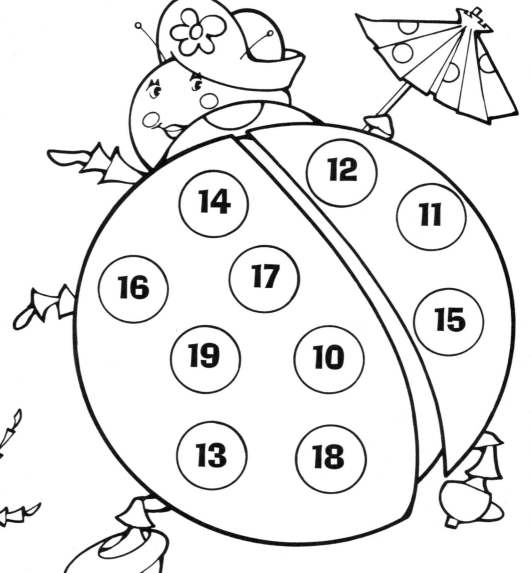

The lucky number is _____.

Name _____ Date _____

Picnic Guest

Help Adam Ant take three different paths to the picnic basket. Begin at each arrow, draw the path with a pencil, and then subtract the numbers along each path, starting with 19. Write your answers in the circles.

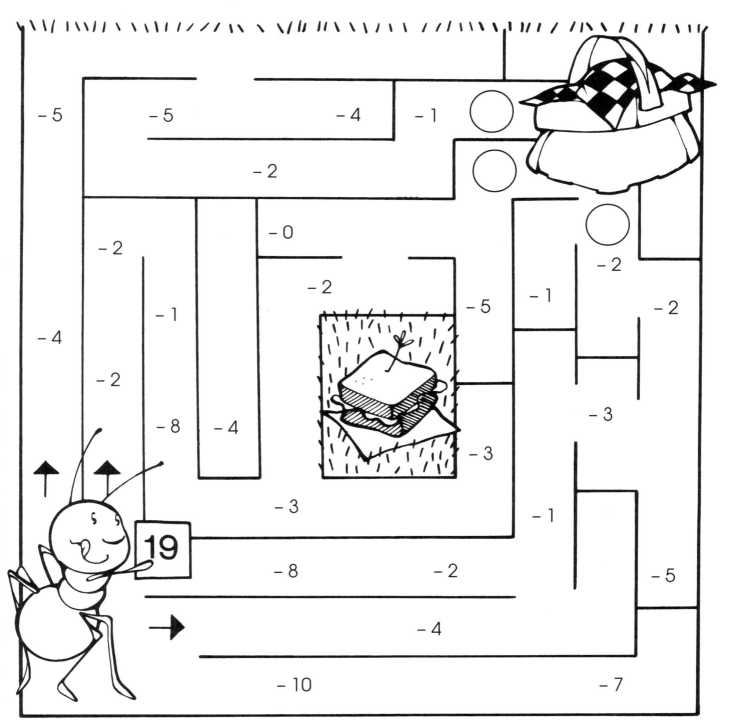

Addition & Subtraction Facts to 20 ©2002 Creative Teaching Press

Name _____ Date _____

Zigzag Differences

Subtract. Draw a line from each answer in column A to the matching answer in column B. Then draw a line from each answer in column B to the matching answer in column C.

Column A	**Column B**	**Column C**
19 – 8 = _____ ●	● 15 – 7 = _____ ●	● 13 – 7 = _____
12 – 4 = _____ ●	● 15 – 6 = _____ ●	● 15 – 4 = _____
12 – 6 = _____ ●	● 7 – 4 = _____ ●	● 16 – 7 = _____
18 – 9 = _____ ●	● 13 – 2 = _____ ●	● 16 – 8 = _____
12 – 9 = _____ ●	● 11 – 5 = _____ ●	● 11 – 8 = _____

Addition & Subtraction Facts to 20 ©2002 Creative Teaching Press

Name _____ Date _____

Tricky Triangles Game

Materials

scissors
game triangles (pages 81 and 82)

How to Play

1. Cut out the triangles. Place a triangle with a face on the table.

2. **Player A:** Place the side of a triangle with an addition problem next to another triangle with the correct sum. Place the problem and sum directly next to each other.

3. **Player B:** Take a turn, matching an addition problem to its sum.

4. Take turns until you make a shape.

What shape did you make? _____

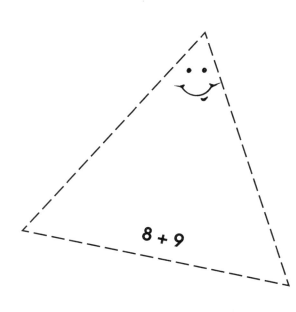

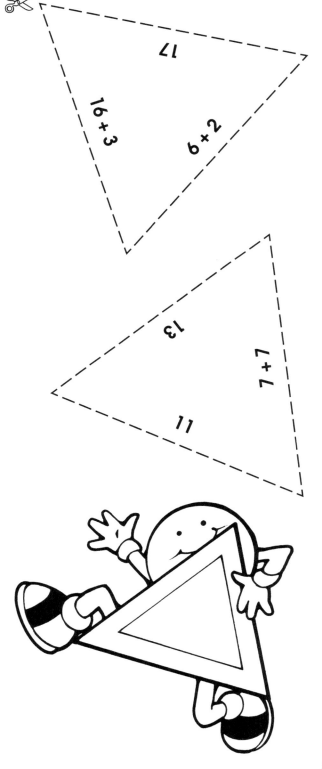

Tricky Triangles Game

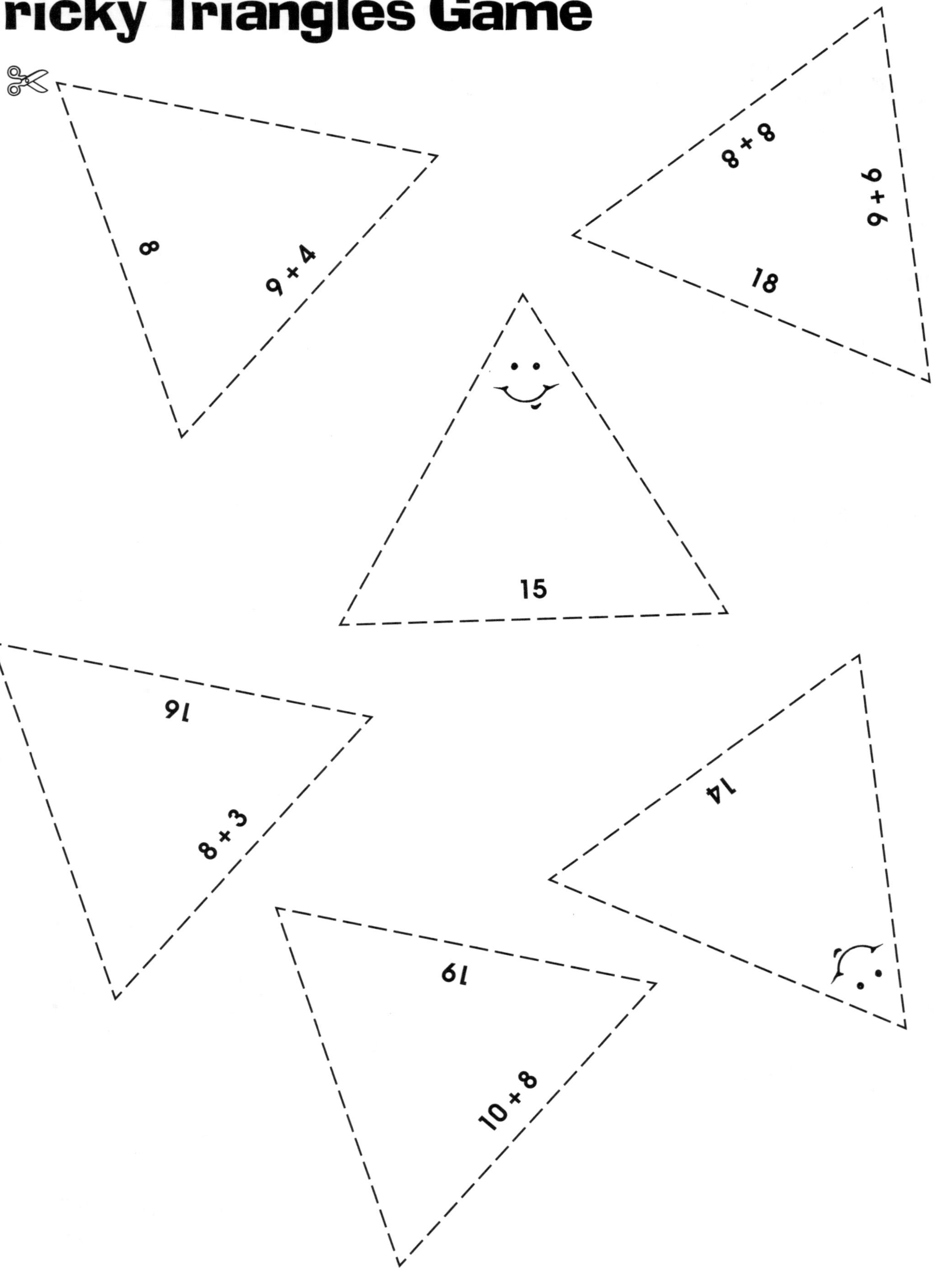

8

9 + 4

8 + 8

9 + 6

18

15

16

8 + 3

14

19

10 + 8

Addition & Subtraction Facts to 20 ©2002 Creative Teaching Press

Name _____ Date _____

Number Scramble 20

Choose two numbers in each group to make
addition sentences. Cross out the two numbers
in each group that you did not use.

Example:

12	✗	**8**	✗

___8___ + ___12___ = 20

___12___ + ___8___ = 20

---

4   8   6   9

_____ + _____ = 13

_____ + _____ = 13

---

5   14   8   12

_____ + _____ = 19

_____ + _____ = 19

---

3   11   7   9

_____ + _____ = 16

_____ + _____ = 16

---

7   9   9   12

_____ + _____ = 18

_____ + _____ = 18

---

13   14   6   8

_____ + _____ = 20

_____ + _____ = 20

---

6   9   8   3

_____ + _____ = 14

_____ + _____ = 14

---

13   6   5   12

_____ + _____ = 19

_____ + _____ = 19

---

7   6   11   8

_____ + _____ = 15

_____ + _____ = 15

---

9   12   8   6

_____ + _____ = 15

_____ + _____ = 15

---

11   9   5   8

_____ + _____ = 17

_____ + _____ = 17

---

13   12   5   7

_____ + _____ = 20

_____ + _____ = 20

Name _____ Date _____

Bear Tracks

Add. Then show the bear's path by coloring all the tracks that have the sum of 20.

Addition & Subtraction Facts to 20 ©2002 Creative Teaching Press

Name _____ Date _____

Super 20 Square

There are 13 subtraction problems in this puzzle.
Circle them. They can go across or down.

Hint: A number can be used in more than
one problem.

19	20	20	0	19
2	18	6	12	12
17	3	14	7	7
16	15	1	5	4
11	7	4	2	3

Name _____ Date _____

Sliding Down

Subtract the numbers down each slide, starting with 20. Then use your answers to break the code and solve the riddle. Match the answers to the numbers in the answer key, and write the letters in order on the lines below.

6	7	8	9	10	11	12	13
I	M	S	O	L	K	C	H

Riddle: What did the swing set say to the slide?

Hi, _____ _____ _____ _____ _____!

Addition & Subtraction Facts to 20 ©2002 Creative Teaching Press

Name _____ Date _____

Crazy Cards Game

Materials
deck of cards
calculator or counting beans

How to Play

1. Shuffle the cards and divide them into two equal piles. Place a pile facedown in front of each player.

   ### Card Values
   Aces = **1**
   Jokers = **0**
   Numbers **2–10** keep their value
   Face Cards = **10**

2. Each player flips over a card and adds the numbers (or values) on the two cards. The first player to say the correct answer aloud takes both cards. If the other player challenges the answer, he or she can check it with a calculator. If the answer is wrong, the challenger takes both cards.

3. Keep playing until all the cards are gone. The player with the most cards wins.

Score Sheet

Player A _____	**Player B** _____
1. _____ + _____ = _____	1. _____ + _____ = _____
2. _____ + _____ = _____	2. _____ + _____ = _____
3. _____ + _____ = _____	3. _____ + _____ = _____
4. _____ + _____ = _____	4. _____ + _____ = _____
5. _____ + _____ = _____	5. _____ + _____ = _____
6. _____ + _____ = _____	6. _____ + _____ = _____
7. _____ + _____ = _____	7. _____ + _____ = _____
8. _____ + _____ = _____	8. _____ + _____ = _____
9. _____ + _____ = _____	9. _____ + _____ = _____
10. _____ + _____ = _____	10. _____ + _____ = _____
Score = _____	Score = _____

Addition & Subtraction Facts to 20 ©2002 Creative Teaching Press

Name _____ Date _____

Addition Quiz: 0 to 10

1. 0 + 0 = _____	**2.** 2 + 5 = _____	**3.** 5 + 3 = _____	**4.** 2 + 2 = _____	**5.** 7 + 3 = _____
6. 4 + 6 = _____	**7.** 4 + 1 = _____	**8.** 5 + 5 = _____	**9.** 2 + 1 = _____	**10.** 2 + 6 = _____
11. 3 + 4 = _____	**12.** 3 + 2 = _____	**13.** 1 + 0 = _____	**14.** 3 + 3 = _____	**15.** 1 + 3 = _____
16. 1 + 1 = _____	**17.** 6 + 3 = _____	**18.** 0 + 3 = _____	**19.** 4 + 2 = _____	**20.** 4 + 5 = _____
21. 6 + 4 = _____	**22.** 5 + 4 = _____	**23.** 4 + 3 = _____	**24.** 1 + 2 = _____	**25.** 4 + 4 = _____

4 8 7 3

2 +

8

Name _____ Date _____

Subtraction Quiz: 10 to 0

1. $8 - 6 =$ ____	2. $9 - 5 =$ ____	3. $10 - 3 =$ ____	4. $3 - 2 =$ ____	5. $6 - 3 =$ ____
6. $9 - 4 =$ ____	7. $10 - 0 =$ ____	8. $9 - 3 =$ ____	9. $10 - 2 =$ ____	10. $10 - 1 =$ ____
11. $8 - 5 =$ ____	12. $10 - 4 =$ ____	13. $7 - 2 =$ ____	14. $6 - 4 =$ ____	15. $8 - 1 =$ ____
16. $7 - 5 =$ ____	17. $10 - 6 =$ ____	18. $7 - 3 =$ ____	19. $8 - 3 =$ ____	20. $10 - 5 =$ ____
21. $8 - 4 =$ ____	22. $5 - 3 =$ ____	23. $4 - 1 =$ ____	24. $5 - 2 =$ ____	25. $10 - 8 =$ ____

$5 - 1$ $6 - 4$ $9 - 0$

Addition Quiz: 11 to 20

1. $11 + 0 =$ _____	2. $6 + 5 =$ _____	3. $8 + 8 =$ _____	4. $9 + 2 =$ _____	5. $7 + 3 =$ _____
6. $10 + 10 =$ _____	7. $9 + 8 =$ _____	8. $7 + 8 =$ _____	9. $8 + 12 =$ _____	10. $14 + 5 =$ _____
11. $9 + 5 =$ _____	12. $6 + 9 =$ _____	13. $10 + 5 =$ _____	14. $6 + 6 =$ _____	15. $6 + 7 =$ _____
16. $8 + 5 =$ _____	17. $7 + 7 =$ _____	18. $9 + 9 =$ _____	19. $9 + 7 =$ _____	20. $8 + 7 =$ _____
21. $9 + 3 =$ _____	22. $7 + 5 =$ _____	23. $10 + 8 =$ _____	24. $6 + 10 =$ _____	25. $13 + 6 =$ _____

Name _____ Date _____

Subtraction Quiz: 20 to 11

1.	2.	3.	4.	5.
19 – 8 = _____	20 – 10 = _____	16 – 8 = _____	12 – 5 = _____	16 – 7 = _____
6.	**7.**	**8.**	**9.**	**10.**
18 – 9 = _____	11 – 2 = _____	17 – 9 = _____	12 – 8 = _____	11 – 3 = _____
11.	**12.**	**13.**	**14.**	**15.**
20 – 0 = _____	14 – 8 = _____	17 – 8 = _____	13 – 6 = _____	19 – 7 = _____
16.	**17.**	**18.**	**19.**	**20.**
13 – 7 = _____	12 – 9 = _____	13 – 4 = _____	11 – 8 = _____	18 – 8 = _____
21.	**22.**	**23.**	**24.**	**25.**
15 – 7 = _____	13 – 5 = _____	15 – 6 = _____	14 – 7 = _____	20 – 5 = _____

12 – 9   20 – 8   5
                  4
                        7

Addition & Subtraction Facts to 20 ©2002 Creative Teaching Press

Answer Key

Page 5

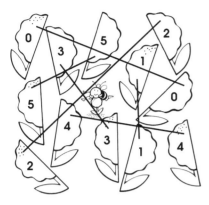

Page 7

Page 9

$$2 + 0 = 2 \qquad 3 + 3 = 6 \qquad 0 + 2 = 2$$
$$3 + 2 = 5 \qquad 1 + 1 = 2 \qquad 5 + 0 = 5$$
$$4 + 2 = 6 \qquad 1 + 4 = 5 \qquad 1 + 5 = 6$$
$$3 + 1 = 4 \qquad 3 + 0 = 3 \qquad 1 + 3 = 4$$
$$2 + 1 = 3 \qquad 2 + 2 = 4 \qquad 1 + 2 = 3$$

Page 10

1. $1 + 2 = 3$
2. $2 + 3 = 5$
3. $1 + 3 = 4$
4. $4 + 1 = 5$
5. $3 + 1 = 4$
6. $1 + 4 = 5$
7. $2 + 2 = 4$
8. $3 + 2 = 5$
9. $2 + 4 = 6$
10. $3 + 3 = 6$

Page 11

Page 13

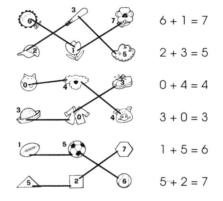

$$6 + 1 = 7$$
$$2 + 3 = 5$$
$$0 + 4 = 4$$
$$3 + 0 = 3$$
$$1 + 5 = 6$$
$$5 + 2 = 7$$

Page 14

"MOO"-VE OVER
HI "NEIGH"-BOR

Page 15

2/5; 4/3; 3/3
1/4; 4/2; 0/4
1/3; 0/1; 3/2
0/3; 1/1; 6/1

Page 18

1. $4 + 3 = 7$
2. $3 + 2 = 5$
3. $3 + 3 = 6$
4. $2 + 5 = 7$
5. $2 + 2 = 4$
6. $4 + 2 = 6$
7. $5 + 2 = 7$
8. $4 + 4 = 8$
9. $5 + 3 = 8$
10. $3 + 5 = 8$

Page 19

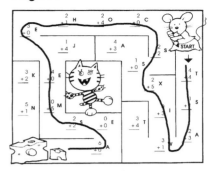

SWISS CHEESE

Page 20

4; 2; 3; 2; 5

Page 21

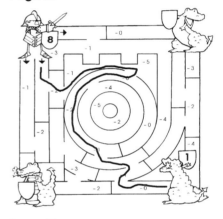

Page 23

HI, WHO IS IT?

Page 24

$9 = 4 + 5, 6 + 3, 2 + 7$
$8 = 3 + 5, 4 + 4$
$7 = 4 + 3, 5 + 2, 6 + 1$
$6 = 3 + 3, 1 + 5, 4 + 2$
$5 = 4 + 1, 5 + 0, 2 + 3$
$4 = 1 + 3, 4 + 0, 2 + 2$

Page 25

4; 8; 3; 5; 7; 6; 9; 0

Page 26

Secret number: 4

Page 28

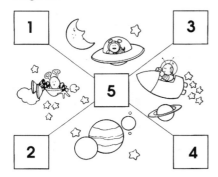

```
1                    3

        5

2                    4
```

Page 29

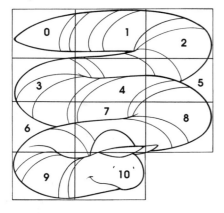

```
0     1
            2
3     4
      5
   7     8
6
9     10
```

Page 30

HE DIDN'T HAVE THE GUTS.

Page 31

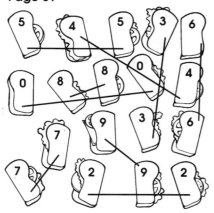

Page 34

The secret number is 7.

Page 35

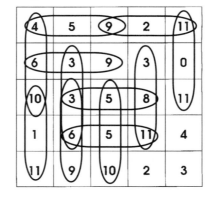

```
4   5   9   2   11
6   3   9   3   0
10  3   5   8   11
1   6   5   11  4
11  9   10  2   3
```

Page 36

HE THOUGHT IT WAS WHEELIE COOL!

Page 39

1. 4 + 6 = 10
2. 6 + 3 = 9
3. 5 + 2 = 7
4. 3 + 4 = 7
5. 4 + 4 = 8
6. 6 + 1 = 7
7. 5 + 4 = 9
8. 6 + 6 = 12
9. 5 + 6 = 11
10. 2 + 4 = 6
11. 5 + 5 = 10
12. 5 + 3 = 8

Page 40

Page 42

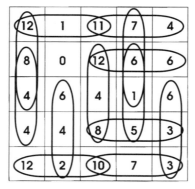

```
12  1   11  7   4
8   0   12  6   6
4   6   4   1   6
4   4   8   5   4
12  2   10  7   3
```

Page 44

IN PIG-UP TRUCKS

Page 45

DO YOU WORK OUT?

Page 46

Page 47

7; 3; 8; 1; 5

Page 50

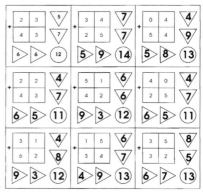

Page 51

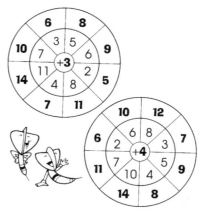

Addition & Subtraction Facts to 20 ©2002 Creative Teaching Press

Page 52

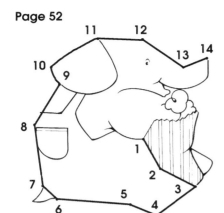

Page 53

Silly Squirrel

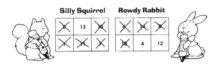

Page 55

There are 13 snakes.

Page 56

Page 57

What letter did you make? __X__

Page 58

Here is one version:

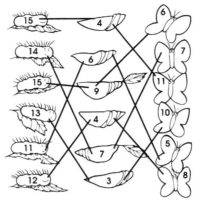

Page 59

8 = 4 + 4, 5 + 3, 6 + 2
10 = 5 + 5, 6 + 4, 7 + 3
13 = 8 + 5, 6 + 7, 11 + 2, 10 + 3
15 = 11 + 4, 10 + 5, 7 + 8

Page 60

11 = 8 + 3, 5 + 6, 5 + 3 + 3
12 = 7 + 5, 9 + 3, 8 + 4, 6 + 6,
    3 + 3 + 6, 1 + 8 + 3, 4 + 5 + 3
14 = 11 + 3, 9 + 5, 8 + 6, 8 + 3 + 3,
    5 + 6 + 3
15 = 9 + 6, 4 + 5 + 6, 6 + 6 + 3,
    8 + 1 + 6, 9 + 3 + 3, 4 + 8 + 3

Page 61

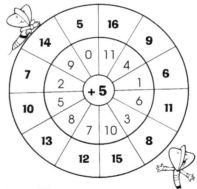

Page 62

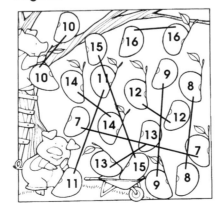

Page 64

9/7; 6/9; 6/4
4/8; 8/5; 7/9
6/8; 5/6; 3/6
8/8; 2/6; 7/8

Page 66

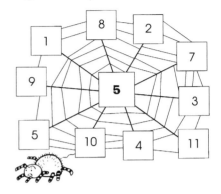

The number 6 is left over.

Page 67

1. 10 + 7 = 17
2. 9 + 7 = 16
3. 6 + 5 = 11
4. 9 + 8 = 17
5. 3 + 10 = 13
6. 7 + 4 = 11
7. 8 + 9 = 17
8. 9 + 4 = 13
9. 6 + 8 = 14
10. 7 + 7 = 14
11. 7 + 5 = 12
12. 6 + 3 = 9

Page 68

IT WAS IN STITCHES.

Page 69

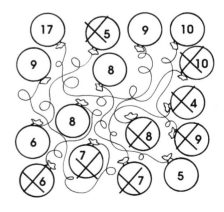

Pages 70–71

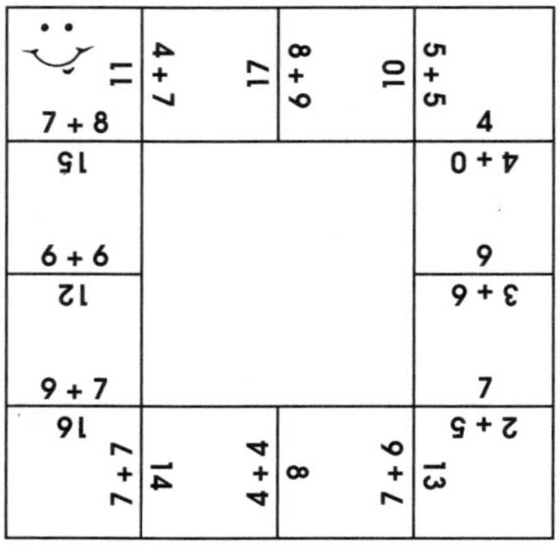

Page 72

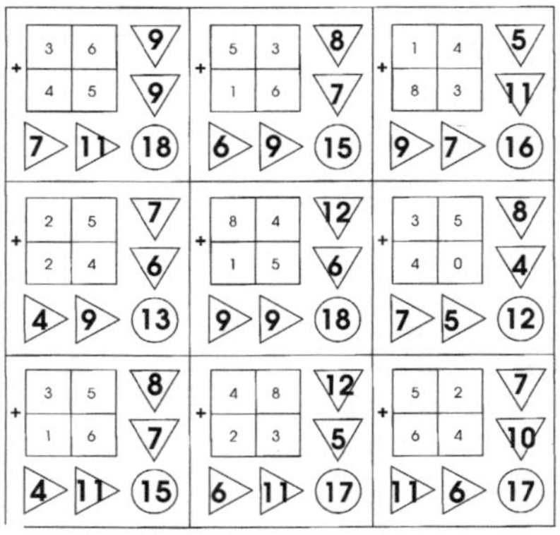

Page 73

CHOCOLATE

Page 74

6 = 15 – 9, 12 – 6, 7 – 1, 13 – 7
4 = 12 – 8, 13 – 9
7 = 15 – 8, 16 – 9, 14 – 7,
13 – 6, 8 – 1, 9 – 2
5 = 13 – 8, 12 – 7, 10 – 5
8 = 9 – 1, 13 – 5, 12 – 4, 15 – 7,
10 – 2
3 = 18 – 15, 12 – 9, 5 – 2
The sum with the most circled sentences is 7.

Page 75

7; 6; 5; 8
Circle the house with 5.

Page 77

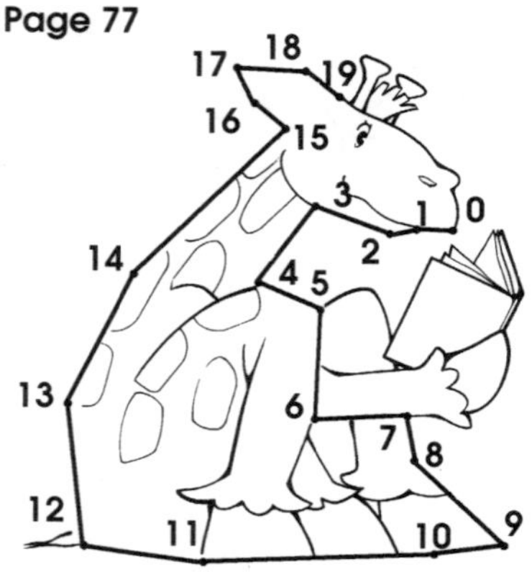

Page 78

The lucky number is 16.

Page 79

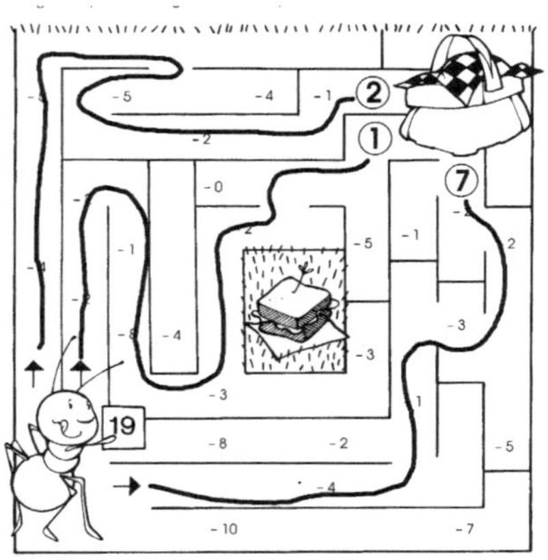

Page 80

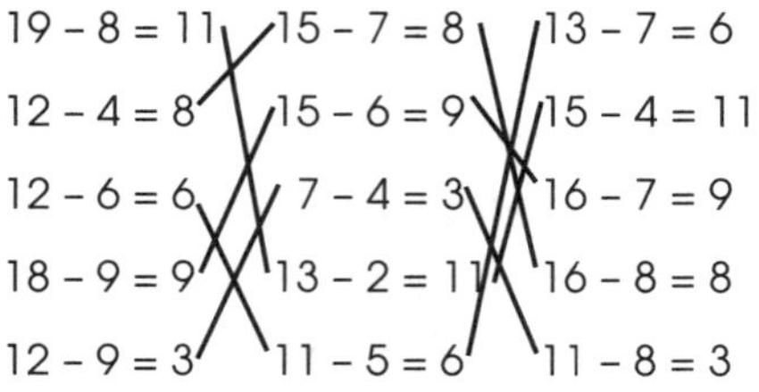
19 – 8 = 11
12 – 4 = 8
12 – 6 = 6
18 – 9 = 9
12 – 9 = 3
15 – 7 = 8
15 – 6 = 9
7 – 4 = 3
13 – 2 = 11
11 – 5 = 6
13 – 7 = 6
15 – 4 = 11
16 – 7 = 9
16 – 8 = 8
11 – 8 = 3

Pages 81–82

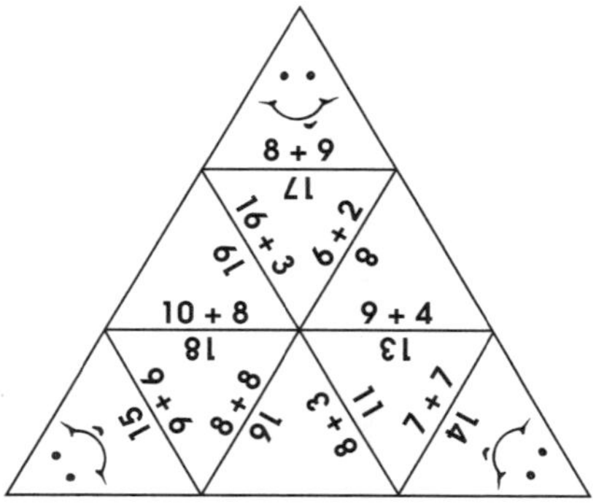

Page 83

12/8; 4/9; 5/14
7/9; 9/9; 14/6
6/8; 13/6; 7/8
9/6; 9/8; 13/7

Page 84

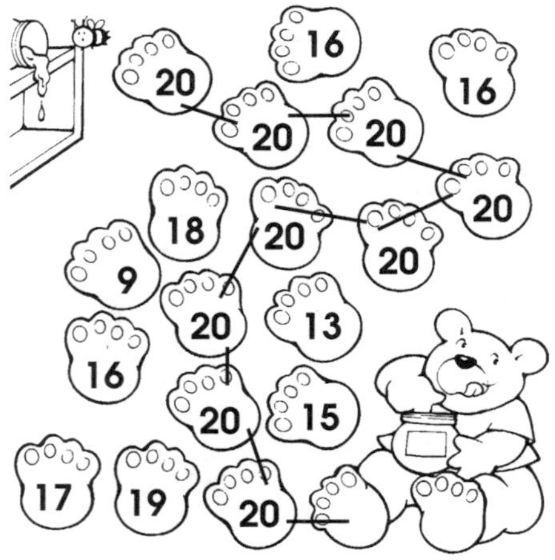

Page 85

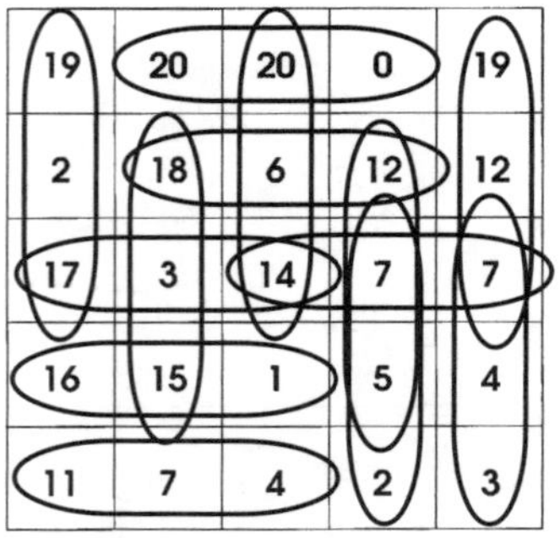
19 20 20 0 19
2 18 6 12 12
17 3 14 7 7
16 15 1 5 4
11 7 4 2 3

Page 86

HI, SLICK!

Page 89

1. 0	2. 7	3. 8	4. 4	5. 10
6. 10	7. 5	8. 10	9. 3	10. 8
11. 7	12. 5	13. 1	14. 6	15. 4
16. 2	17. 9	18. 3	19. 6	20. 9
21. 10	22. 9	23. 7	24. 3	25. 8

Page 90

1. 2	2. 4	3. 7	4. 1	5. 3
6. 5	7. 10	8. 6	9. 8	10. 9
11. 3	12. 6	13. 5	14. 2	15. 7
16. 2	17. 4	18. 4	19. 5	20. 5
21. 4	22. 2	23. 3	24. 3	25. 2

Page 91

1. 11	2. 11	3. 16	4. 11	5. 10
6. 20	7. 17	8. 15	9. 20	10. 19
11. 14	12. 15	13. 15	14. 12	15. 13
16. 13	17. 14	18. 18	19. 16	20. 15
21. 12	22. 12	23. 18	24. 16	25. 19

Page 92

1. 11	2. 10	3. 8	4. 7	5. 9
6. 9	7. 9	8. 8	9. 4	10. 8
11. 20	12. 6	13. 9	14. 7	15. 12
16. 6	17. 3	18. 9	19. 3	20. 10
21. 8	22. 8	23. 9	24. 7	25. 15

Addition & Subtraction Facts to 20 ©2002 Creative Teaching Press